designing for the social web

joshua porter

New Riders

VOICES THAT MATTER™

Designing for the Social Web
Joshua Porter

New Riders
1249 Eighth Street
Berkeley, CA 94710
510/524-2178
510/524-2221 (fax)

Find us on the Web at www.newriders.com
To report errors, please send a note to errata@peachpit.com

New Riders is an imprint of Peachpit, a division of Pearson Education

Project Editor: Michael J. Nolan
Development Editor: Margaret Anderson/Stellarvisions
Production Editor: Kate Reber
Technical Editor: Christina Wodtke
Proofreader: Rose Weisburd
Indexer: FireCrystal Communications
Book design: Mimi Heft
Compositor: WolfsonDesign
Cover design: Michael J. Nolan/Aren Howell

ISBN 13: 978-0-321-53492-7
ISBN 10: 0-321-53492-1

9 8 7 6 5 4 3 2 1

Printed and bound in the United States of America

Acknowledgements

Like many people, I've always wanted to write a book. Growing up reading my favorites—*Sherlock Holmes, The Lord of the Rings,* and *The Great Gatsby*— I thought that writing would be a great adventure, a grand experiment. After all, that's what reading was! Wouldn't writing be even better?

Well, now I've written one. And while I wrote a book on web design and not the great American novel, I now know more about the process I always wondered about. It turns out to be a whole bunch of hard work, extremely long hours, coupled with the emotional ups and downs of a Red Sox season (as if I needed more than one per year). But extremely satisfying in the end.

I want to thank my development editor Margaret Anderson, who seemed to know exactly how to manage me during the project (and I need management!). Her encouragement and guidance means a tremendous amount to me.

And Michael Nolan and the rest of the folks at New Riders, who believed in me even when the outline of my book was in shambles. You supported me even when I had no momentum. Thank you.

My technical editor Christina Wodtke, whom I chose not only for her knowledge of the domain, but because she is as honest a person as I know. Your intellectual curiosity is truly amazing.

Seth Godin, who consistently publishes small blog posts that have a big impact, including this one (http://sethgodin.typepad.com/the_dip/2007/04/not_settling.html), which was the final push I needed to pursue my passion and go out on my own.

Clay Shirky, whose wonderful writing about the web got me blogging in the first place.

Howard Rheingold, whom I rediscovered and found incredibly prescient on all social topics related to the web.

Luke Wroblewski, who is a wonderful writer and teacher of design.

Steve Krug, whose book *Don't Make Me Think* set the bar for books in the web genre.

Andrew Chak, whose under-appreciated book *Submit Now: Designing Persuasive Web Sites* was a big influence in my thinking about social design.

To bloggers everywhere, who write out of love for what they do, who share their knowledge with the world while asking for little in return. People ask me what's the last book I read. I answer, "I have no idea ... but I've read tens of thousands of blog posts in the last few years. Does that count?."

To my readers at Bokardo, who have given me the impression that this was all worth it, who have pushed back on me when I did or said something silly, and have encouraged me to do great things. I have lots more in store for you folks. :)

To my clients who I put off while writing the book. I thank you for your patience ... now let's get building great things!

I also want to thank those folks who gave me advice and direction during the writing of the book over not just the last eight months of writing, but over the last few years. They may not have known they were doing so, but they were immensely valuable.

Dan Cederholm, Thomas Vander Wal, Gerry McGovern, Andy Budd, Jeffrey Zeldman, Molly Holzschlag, and Eric Meyer.

I want to thank professor Bill Hart-Davidson for countless insightful conversations over the years. You have been a wonderful mentor and friend.

And I must thank many times over the folks I have worked with at UIE: Jared Spool, Christine Perfetti, Will Schroeder, Donna Fowler, David Brittan, Andy Bourland, Jason Marcoux, Ashley McKee, and Brian Christiansen. Jared's knowledge of usability and Christine's dedication to doing great work are ongoing inspirations to me.

I want to thank my family, whose quiet support I've had with me not only through writing the book, but through my whole life. It's easy to live and be happy with a sister, brother, and parents like I have.

Ed Giblin, my father-in-law, who has helped tremendously over the last year.

And most importantly I must thank my love Alana, who had more patience than one could possibly hope for while writing a book. Having a fan like her is the only thing a guy needs ... well ... to do anything in the world. She not only kept me moving forward but was a perfect mother of our daughter as well. Now let's play!

Table of Contents

Introduction

Getting back to connectedness

"During [the twentieth] century we have for the first time been dominated by non-interactive forms of entertainment: cinema, radio, recorded music and television. Before they came along all entertainment was interactive: theatre, music, sport—the performers and audience were there together, and even a respectfully silent audience exerted a powerful shaping presence on the unfolding of whatever drama they were there for. We didn't need a special word for interactivity in the same way that we don't (yet) need a special word for people with only one head.

I expect that history will show 'normal' mainstream twentieth century media to be the aberration in all this. 'Please, miss, you mean they could only just sit there and watch? They couldn't do anything? Didn't everybody feel terribly isolated or alienated or ignored?'

'Yes, child, that's why they all went mad. Before the Restoration.'

'What was the Restoration again, please, miss?'

'The end of the twentieth century, child. When we started to get interactivity back.'"[1]

DOUGLAS ADAMS, WRITING IN 1999

---

1   From one of my all-time favorites: How to Stop Worrying and Love the Internet, by Douglas Adams: http://www.douglasadams.com/dna/19990901-00-a.html

It's odd to think of the twentieth century as somehow less interactive than other periods in history. But, in terms of how we spent most of our time, it was. Our TVs and radios and automobiles served to distance us from each other. It's possible, for instance, to ride around in a car, see everyone in town, yet never say "hello." How many of us sit at home and watch TV instead of going out and socializing?

When I started to write this book on designing for the social web, I thought I would be talking about new ideas that we hadn't really dealt with before. In my work as a web designer, I had been challenged with many interesting projects, building everything from restaurant review sites to social networking applications. It turns out that the design of this software is new, but the principles underlying its success are as old as humanity.

Part Interface Design, Part Psychology

The principles on which successful social software is built are the basics of human psychology. People use software to do all the same things they used to do without it: talk with each other, form groups, gain respect, manage their lives, have fun.

To web designers, tasked with creating increasingly sophisticated applications, it can seem daunting to get into these psychological issues. How do you not only make services personally valuable with easy-to-use interfaces, but also support people's social desires for interactivity, authority, reputation, identity, and control?

I wrote this book to begin the discussion. And in writing it, I went deep into social psychology research to try to uncover ideas and explanations that we can use in design. But even though I have tried to share many important and interesting ideas, I have barely begun to uncover an amazing wealth of research.

We are just at the beginning of knowing how to design for a networked world.

What's in the Book

I start off in Chapter 1, The Rise of the Social Web, with a discussion of the scale and significance of the social web phenomenon. Chapter 2, A Framework for Social Design, describes a prioritization scheme called the AOF method that helps designers make early decisions about what features their software should have.

The rest of the book examines the series of design problems that correspond to increasing involvement—the *Usage Lifecycle*—and the strategies social web design can offer. The concept of the usage lifecycle is central to understanding the book.

The Usage Lifecycle

There is a common set of hurdles that every web site faces. No matter if a site is selling books or providing a tool to manage contacts or supporting a social network, there is a general lifecycle people go through in order to use its software.

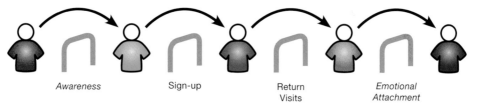

Awareness   Sign-up   Return Visits   *Emotional Attachment*

Unaware	**Interested**	**First-time Use**	**Regular Use**	**Passionate Use**
This very large group includes everyone out there who has never seen your web site or read about your software.	People who are interested in your software have lots of questions and need an explanation of benefits before taking the plunge.	People using your software for the first time are at a critical juncture. It is here that they decide whether or not to have a relationship with you.	People who use your software regularly feel that they're getting value from it. Promoting a sense of efficacy is important to gaining their passion.	Passionate participants are the ultimate goal. They are your best supporters, as they freely share their knowledge about you and your software.

The Usage Lifecycle is a set of stages people go through when using software. The hurdles that separate the stages are the major challenges faced in getting to the next stage. By recognizing that people are at different stages and have different hurdles to overcome, you can better make design decisions targeted at those stages.

The Five Stages of the Usage Lifecycle

There are five stages to the usage lifecycle and four major hurdles.

1. Unaware

In the beginning stage, most people are unaware of your software, but they *are* aware of their own frustrations with their current way of doing things. Addressing their biggest pain points and telling an authentic story is crucial to getting their attention.

Awareness

Unaware   Interested

We talk about getting over the Awareness hurdle in Chapter 3, Authentic Conversations.

2. Interested

People at this stage have heard about your site from a friend, a news story, a blog post, or followed a link, and become interested. They are ready to hear more about what you offer. They have questions. They are ready for you to tell them what they want to hear. If you can do that, they'll gladly sign up.

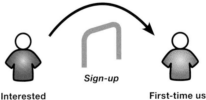

Sign-up

Interested   First-time use

We talk about getting over the Sign-up hurdle in Chapter 4, Design for Sign-up.

3. First-time Use

People at this stage are using your software for the first time. As these people settle into using your app, they're making judgments about its long-term value. Do they find it easy to get up to speed? Does the software keep the promises you made? They are assessing whether this site is really for them, and worth switching from what they currently have.

First-time use is a crucial step for keeping momentum. If people don't see the value in your service and fall off here, they may never return.

Return visits

First-time use   **Regular use**

We talk about getting over the
Return Visits hurdle in Chapter 5,
Design for Ongoing Participation.

4. Regular Use

People at this stage are regularly using your software. This is where you start having success as people spend significant time learning and using. Not only do these people start telling others about your service, but they'll start having conversations with you that you can learn from.

In Chapter 6, Design for Collective Intelligence, I talk about complex adaptive systems like Digg, which are an interesting case of persistent and constantly changing use.

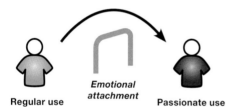

Emotional attachment

Regular use   **Passionate use**

Many of the strategies in
Chapter 5 and 6, if effectively
implemented, can create
passionate use.

5. Passionate Use

Emotional attachment usually happens only after software achieves real success. This is what separates eBay, Amazon, Craigslist and other super successes: their audiences are *passionate* about using them. These people say things like "I love Amazon" and "eBay is the bomb."

And now we come to why this is a cycle and not simply a progression. Passionate people are the key to driving new usage of your site, as they bring others into the fold by evangelizing your service.

Chapter 7, Design for Sharing, addresses a specific way to empower this passionate audience.

In Chapter 8, The Funnel Analysis, we begin measuring the effectiveness of your web application and actually show the results of your work.

What makes a hurdle?

As people move through the stages in the usage lifecycle, they clear hurdles along the way. The hurdles are significant because they mean a change in behavior is necessary.

1. **They have to pay attention.**
2. **They have to make a decision.** Do they sign up for the service or not?
3. **They have to input personal information.** This is about trust. Does the person trust your software (i.e. *you*)? Do they feel right adding all their friends to this application?
4. **They have to pay money.**
5. **They are making a decision for someone else.** Often we are much more careful when deciding on something that our job relies on.
6. **They have to give up their current way of doing things.** Every time someone uses new software they're also giving up their old software.

One Goal: Better Design

I have had one goal in writing this book: to help you design better social web sites. If your site improves as the result of reading this book, then I have done my job.

However, I realize it can be quite overwhelming to add yet another discipline, psychology, to the vast array of activities we already do as designers. But in some ways that is what must happen if we are to truly understand why people do what they do when using social software.

But I do think there might be a higher outcome as well. If we begin to consider the underlying motivations of people, putting ourselves in their shoes, we might come to feel more empathy toward not only the people we design for, but everyone else in our lives as well. Is that too idealistic? Perhaps so, but nothing great was ever accomplished as the result of low expectations. Enjoy the book!

The Rise of the Social Web

A social and economic change that has barely begun

"The Web is more a social creation than a technical one. I designed it for a social effect—to help people work together—and not as a technical toy. The ultimate goal of the Web is to support and improve our weblike existence in the world. We clump into families, associations, and companies. We develop trust across the miles and distrust around the corner. What we believe, endorse, agree with, and depend on is representable and, increasingly, represented on the Web. We all have to ensure that the society we build with the Web is of the sort we intend."

—TIM BERNERS-LEE, WEAVING THE WEB[1]

---

1 http://www.w3.org/People/Berners-Lee/Weaving/

The Amazon Effect

If you've ever watched someone shop at Amazon.com, you may have witnessed the Amazon Effect.

I first saw the Amazon Effect during a usability study several years ago. I was observing a person shopping for a digital camera recommended to her by a friend. As part of the testing procedure, I asked the shopper to go to CircuitCity.com and try to buy the camera. She started typing the URL, then stopped.

> **Shopper:** *Can I go to Amazon first?*
>
> **Me:** *No.*
>
> **Shopper (frowning):** *Well, I always go to Amazon first. I love Amazon.*

Unfortunately, our testing methodology didn't allow for that. We couldn't let people shop just anywhere. We were testing very specific sites at the request of our client. Though we were testing Amazon in the study, we weren't testing Amazon with this particular shopper.

> **Me:** *I'm sorry. I can't let you go there just now. But let me ask: why do you want to go to Amazon?*

Up to that point, we'd had a couple of people ask to visit Amazon in the test and had assumed they kept asking because they had accounts there. We figured they had previously shopped at Amazon and had a history with the company, had created wish lists and purchase histories there, and were generally more comfortable shopping in a familiar environment. We assumed the familiarity of Amazon was what kept them coming back.

But as with so many assumptions, it was wrong.

> **Shopper:** *I go to Amazon to do research on a product I'm shopping for, even when I plan to buy it on another site.*
>
> **Me:** *Even when you plan to buy it on another site?*
>
> **Shopper:** *Yes, of course.*

Wow! This wasn't what we had expected. People wanted to go to Amazon so badly to do *product research*, not because they had an account there. The magnetic pull of Amazon, what I like to call the *Amazon Effect*, was entirely different from what we had assumed.

People-Powered Research

So why the pull of Amazon versus, say, another online electronics retailer? Didn't Amazon have the same information as other sites? Weren't they basically all selling the same cameras? What does Amazon do that others don't?

The answer becomes clear almost immediately when watching someone shopping: *customer reviews.*

At Amazon, customer reviews act like a magnet, pulling people down the page. That's the content people want. The page loads, the viewer starts to scroll. They keep scrolling until they hit the reviews, which in some cases are up to 6000 pixels down from the top of the page! Nobody seems to mind. They simply scroll through screens and screens of content until they find what they're looking for.

During a test a few days later, another shopper exhibited a distinctive behavior. He went to the reviews and immediately sorted them to bring the 1-star reviews to the top of the list. This meant they wanted to see the negative reviews first.

> **Me:** *Why did you do that?*
>
> **Shopper:** *Well, I want to make sure I'm not buying a lemon.*

Another shopper, who exhibited the same behavior of going directly for the reviews, told me why they rarely look at the other content on the page — the wealth of content like the manufacturer's description and other product information.

> **Shopper:** *I already know what it's going to say, it's going to tell me how great their product is. Why would I need to read that? If I want to know the truth, I have to read what other people like me thought about it.*

There it was: a crystallization of the value of customer reviews. Customer reviews allow people to learn about a product from the experience of others without any potentially biased seller information. *No wonder*

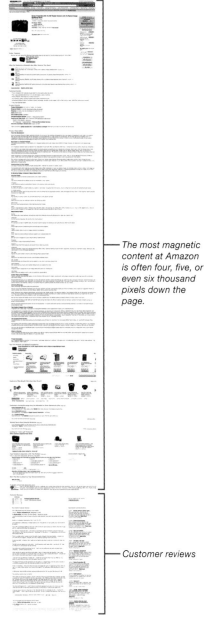

The most magnetic content at Amazon is often four, five, or even six thousand pixels down the page.

Customer reviews

Figure 1.1 Amazon's product pages are extremely long, but that doesn't keep people from scrolling almost the entire length of them to find the customer reviews.

everyone wanted to shop at Amazon. They had information that no other site had: they had *the Truth*.

And that truth, interestingly enough, arose from simply aggregating the conversation of normal people like you and me.

Counter-Intuitive Economics

Let's take a bird's-eye view of what's happening at Amazon. Consider these peculiarities:

▸ **Amazon doesn't always provide the most valuable information on their site.** Instead, the people writing reviews contribute valuable information others are looking for. Amazon simply provides the tool with which to write the reviews.

▸ **People write reviews without getting paid.** There is no monetary reward for writing reviews. Yet dozens of reviewers have written over a thousand reviews each! These folks know they aren't going to get paid, but do it anyway.

▸ **People are not being managed in any tangible way.** This incredible outpouring of reviews is not being managed. Individuals are acting independently of one another and together provide an amazing resource.

▸ **People pay attention to strangers they'll never meet.** Yet, they still take the time to help out these strangers by describing their experience with a product.

▸ **People police each other.** In addition to taking the time to write reviews, people also help judge whether they found a given review helpful, thereby weeding out the bad (by pushing them to the bottom).

▸ **People openly identify themselves.** Even in this most public of places, where anybody could see what they're doing, most people freely identify themselves.

Given our common conception of how to get people to do work, many of these points are counter-intuitive. We've been taught that hard work is rewarded by an honest wage, yet people at Amazon are working for free. People aren't *supposed* to work for free. The value of customer reviews flies in the face of how economics is supposed to work!

The models that economists have created assume there must be an incentive for production, in plain terms *money*. So how could Amazon create such a large, stable, *valuable* system without paying any of their contributors even a penny for their efforts?

The conclusion we must reach is staring us in the face:

Amazon's reviews are about much more than money.

Indeed, the overwhelming success of Amazon's reviews is evidence of a way in which the web has produced a dramatic change in the world's economy. In traditional economic terms the mere existence of reviews just doesn't compute. Few existing economic models can accurately describe the value being given (or received) on Amazon.

Yochai Benkler, author of *Wealth of Networks*, a wonderful book describing these new economic changes in detail, notes:

> A new model of production has taken root; one that should not be there, at least according to our most widely held beliefs about economic behavior.
>
> It should not, the intuitions of the late-twentieth-century American would say, be the case that thousands of volunteers will come together to collaborate...
>
> It certainly should not be that these volunteers will beat the largest and best-financed business enterprises in the world at their own game.
>
> And yet, this is precisely what is happening...[2]

The Social Web

Of course Amazon isn't the only one designing for and supporting the activity of its audience in this way: it is merely one of countless examples of social design on the web. For the purposes of this book, we define social design in the following way:

Definition: Social design is the conception, planning, and production of web sites and applications that support social interaction

---

[2]   Yochai Benkler, *The Wealth of Networks*. Yale University Press, 2006.

We've barely seen the tip of the iceberg when it comes to designing social software. I'm confident we'll be discussing social software (and how to design it) for decades to come. It is the future of the web. Here are several reasons why:

1. **Humans are innately social.** Since humans are social, it makes sense that our software will be social, too.

2. **Social software is a forced move.** The sheer amount of information and choice we're faced with forces us toward authentic conversations (and tools to help us find and have them).

3. **Social software is accelerating.** Social software is trending upward: it is already the fastest growing and most widely used software on the web. The future suggests more of the same.

Let's take a look at each of these reasons in depth to get a clearer picture of the rise of the social web.

Humans Are Innately Social

Humans are innately social creatures. We exhibit *social behavior*. If we did not, if we weren't social from the day we are born, then social software would be incongruous: it just wouldn't make sense. Instead of garnering our attention and energy, Amazon, eBay, and MySpace would be worthless.

While most of us would agree that we are social by nature, what exactly does it mean to be social? Well, *social* is a fuzzy term, and most dictionaries define it as something to do with "group formation" or "living together."[3] But those terms don't illustrate the richness of our social lives. Being social is more than merely forming groups: it's all the interactions, decisions, and conversations that happen in and around those groups!

It includes, but certainly isn't limited to:

Sharing, caring, feeding, loving, fighting, conversing, friendship, sex, envy, shouting, arguing, betrayal, rumor mongering, gossiping, laughing, crying, providing support, whining, advocating for others, recommending, swearing off.

---

3   For example, the dictionary on my Mac says: "of or relating to the aggregate of people living together in a more or less ordered community" (this is not very helpful).

Key Aspects of Social Behavior

1. Humans are complex social animals who interact with each other for almost every need: food and water, shelter, technology, friendship, learning, fun, sex, ritual, sport

2. Humans organize themselves into groups, often belonging to multiple groups at the same time

3. Groups can be as small as two people or as large as a religion, and can be for any purpose

4. Groups can be made up of family, friends, acquaintances, or any set of people with something in common

5. Humans act as both group members and individuals at the same time

6. Humans behave differently in groups than they do individually, and vice-versa

7. Humans play different roles in different parts and periods of their lives

8. When humans are uncertain, they rely on social connections to help them out

9. People usually compare themselves to those in their social group, not to society at large

10. The people we know greatly influence how we act

11. Sometimes being self-interested means to support the group, sometimes it means to diverge from the group and focus on oneself

12. Humans aren't always rational, but usually behave in a self-interested manner

13. Unpredictable behavior emerges within groups over time

14. People derive enormous value from social interaction that cannot be accounted for in monetary terms

Lewin's Equation

The mere fact that we as humans organize ourselves into groups isn't all that special. After all, other animals form groups. But as this list shows, being in groups, and being around groups, and *not being in groups* really changes the way we behave.

We didn't always think this way. In 1933, German behavioral psychologist Kurt Lewin, escaping Hitler's rise to power, emigrated to America in order to continue his studies on group behavior. At that time, the commonly held notion about human behavior was that we act according to our personality. Sigmund Freud and his theories on the unconscious mind were in vogue. Most of the prevailing research assumed in one way or another that our inborn tendencies dictated our behavior.

But Lewin's research said different. He challenged the prevailing wisdom by formulating a simple yet profound statement to describe human behavior. The statement, which was expressed as an equation, of all things, thrust Lewin to the forefront of an emerging field. Indeed, Lewin is often called "the father of social psychology."

This is Lewin's equation:

$B = f(P,E)$

The equation says that an individual's behavior is a function of both their personality *and* their environment. While the classic nature vs. nurture debate asks you to take sides, Lewin's equation does not: it invitingly allows for both the person and their environment to affect what happens in a complex, yet profound, way.

From Environment to Interface Design

Lewin's equation highlights the tension between the individual and the environment. The environment, of course, is basically made up of everything that *isn't* us. That's an awfully big set of things to think about! However, we easily recognize several types of environments. One is the *physical environment*, which has a tremendous effect on what we do. When it's cold outside, we must put clothes on or suffer the consequences.

Other people and groups make up our *social* environment. And, perhaps even as much as the weather dictates how we dress, the actions of others affect how we behave. Imagine how many of our decisions are strongly influenced by what other people say or do. Just as the friend who made a product recommendation to our shopper on Amazon influenced her behavior, so we are profoundly influenced by the people we know and the groups we join.

In the software world there is even another kind of environment: the *software interface.*

The interface is the environment in which people work and play on the web. It is the arbiter of all the communication and interaction that takes place there. If there is an action available in an interface, then you can perform the action. If an action is not available in an interface, then you're out of luck. While we are intuitively aware of this, just as we are aware of the weather, we rarely reflect on how much our behavior is determined by the interfaces we use. Almost all of it!

This sounds like the designers of the interface are in control! Not so fast. Designing an interface that evokes the desired behavior is a huge challenge.

If the interface is too confining, people won't use it.

If the interface is too flexible, people won't know how to use it.

In the middle, the sweet spot, interface designers can create powerful social software that supports the person and their personality, *as well as* the social environment and the groups they are a part of.

The Challenge of Social Software

Thus the challenge of social software is to design interfaces that support the current and desired social behavior of the people who use them.

Designing an effective interface has always been tough, even when we were merely designing interfaces for one person to interact with content we controlled. But when we add the social aspect, things get even more difficult. Though we can see glimpses, we have little understanding of the overall effect of social software going forward. In 1985, Howard Rheingold, writing about the nascent personal computer revolution, foresaw social software's massive challenge and potential for change:

> Nobody knows whether this will turn out to be the best or the worst thing the human race has done for itself, because the outcome of this empowerment will depend in large part on how we react to it and what we choose to do with it. The human mind is not going to be replaced by a machine, at least not in the foreseeable future, but there is little doubt that the worldwide availability of fantasy amplifiers, intellectual toolkits, and interactive electronic communities will change the way people think, learn, and communicate.[4]

Just as humans are social, so our software must be as well.

---

4   Howard Rheingold's books are wonderful: Tools for Thought (http://www.rheingold.com/texts/tft/) and Virtual Communities (http://www.rheingold.com/vc/book/). Though they were written in 1985 and 1993, respectively, they were *at least* a decade ahead of their time. Probably two.

Social Software is a Forced Move

The person shopping at Amazon in the opening of this chapter was relying on social connections to help her make a shopping decision.

She did this in two ways:

First, she asked a friend to recommend a digital camera. That friend, knowing her and her lifestyle, would recommend a camera based on his knowledge of her. Maybe the friend recommended a camera he had experience with. Or, perhaps a different model based on some difference he recognized between them.

Second, the person relied on an informal social network of people at Amazon who wrote reviews. She didn't know these people, yet she relied on them anyway, trusting them to deliver quality information. The trust in this case is present not because they are friends, as was true for the original recommendation, but because they represent the shared experience of shopping for a camera.

This study was merely the first time this phenomenon became clear to me. Since then, I have noted it in nearly all aspects of life. Voting, shopping, eating, reading, computing, driving… in these and all activities we ask others for help in making decisions. Relying on social networks is how the vast majority of decisions are made!

A Forced Move

This reliance on our social network is increasingly a *forced move*. Living in the *Information Age*, for all its benefits and wonders, is like drinking from a fire-hose. We have more information than we know what to do with, more than we could ever digest, and probably more than we can even imagine.

And a previous age, the *Industrial Age*, still has a strong effect as well. The ease of manufacturing at a large scale has caused a situation where we simply have far too many *things* to choose from. So now we not only have too much information, we have too many products as well. Often we don't have two or three options to choose from: we have *dozens*. And then there is a seemingly infinite amount of information about those products! There is simply not enough time to consider each option thoroughly.

To fight this deluge of information, we're turning more and more to trusted sources, whether they be in our own household or in other social circles. Instead of trying to sort, filter, and weed through endless sources of information, we're focusing our attention on those we already trust, or those we have reason to believe might be trusted. We don't have much choice.

The Paradox of Choice

Barry Schwartz notes an interesting side effect of this problem: the Paradox of Choice.[5] He has found that when faced with such an overload we not only fail to make the right choice in many situations, but we often actually get paralyzed and make no choice at all! I remember a friend of mine was shopping for a digital camera several years ago, and decided to utilize several online price trackers to help him find the best model at the best price. He became paralyzed by the options. The paradox was realized: he ended up not getting a camera! He had to rationalize this by citing another reason (a change in financial situation) because on the surface, like any paradox, not choosing due to too much information seems irrational. It's not. It's human.

Ads, Ads, and more Ads

Another continuing effect of the Industrial Age is advertising, which is necessitated as the distance between the person with the message (often a business owner) and the person receiving the message (often a customer) grows. If you have a relationship with the person you're doing business with, your conversation with them (and their ability to help you) is all the advertising they need. But in an age where there is no personal relationship, no face-to-face contact, business owners need to get their message to customers in some other way, and that way is advertising.

Advertisers are always working harder to get our attention. It is said the average person sees anywhere from 500 to 3000 ads each day[6] and an average twenty-year-old has watched 30,000 hours of television.[7] It's hard to go anywhere and not see a plethora of advertisements: a few hours casual use of the web and TV per day and you'll easily see hundreds of advertisements.

---

5   Barry Schwartz, *The Paradox of Choice*. Harper Perennial, 2005.

6   There is considerable debate about how many ads people see per day, with the key issue being how many we notice vs. how many come into our peripheral vision. See more: http://answers.google.com/answers/threadview?id=56750

7   http://www.firstmonday.org/issues/issue2_4/goldhaber/index.html

Bias, Bias, and more Bias

The problem with advertisements isn't just that they're distracting, it's that they're also *biased*: they don't represent a truthful view of the world. They're all about sell, sell, sell. When we see an advertisement, we're seeing an idealistic vision of the world that simply doesn't exist.

As the shopper on Amazon said in reference to the camera manufacturer: "I already know what they're going to say." This bias is simply unacceptable. To retain our sanity in a world of too many biased messages, we're being forced to rely on our social circles to give us sorely needed unbiased perspective. We'll go out of our way for an authentic conversation with someone we can trust. We don't want to know how excited someone is to tell us about *their* great new thing, we want to hear what *people like us* have to say. Just like the Amazon shopper.

The Attention Economy

Combine the increased number of items to choose from, the blitz of advertising, and the explosive growth of the web, and it's easy to see why we are swimming in information. Humans have never had to deal with such a situation.

In 1971, seeing the writing on the wall (and everywhere else), the insightful Herbert Simon described the inevitable outcome of this information onslaught:

> In an information-rich world, the wealth of information means a dearth of something else: a scarcity of whatever it is that information consumes. What information consumes is rather obvious: it consumes the attention of its recipients. Hence a wealth of information creates a poverty of attention and a need to allocate that attention efficiently among the overabundance of information sources that might consume it[8]

Simon points to the real need here: we need to allocate our attention efficiently. In other words, we need to pay attention to what matters, and try to ignore what doesn't.

The *Attention Economy*, as it has come to be called, is all about the exchange of attention in a world where it is increasingly scarce. Much of what we do on the web is about this exchange of attention. To circle back to the reviews at Amazon, it is definitely about more than money: it's about *attention*.

---

8   http://en.wikipedia.org/wiki/Attention_economy

At its very core, social software is about connecting people virtually who already have relationships in the physical world. That's why MySpace and Facebook are so popular. What do most people do on those sites when they sign up? They immediately connect with friends they already have![9] Or, to put it another way, they maintain their current attention streams. These applications are helping people manage their attention in an economy where it is increasingly hard to do so.

When we join social network sites and focus our attention mostly on the people we know there or give our attention to people like us on Amazon, we're filtering information and being parsimonious with our most precious asset. We're effectively saying "No" to the vast majority of information out there, and we're being forced to do this by the sheer amount of information we face.

Social Software is Accelerating

Social software has always been successful. Email, which dates from the early 1960s and is arguably the most successful software ever, was actually used to help build the Internet.[10] Email is social, as it allows you to send messages to one or more people at a time. In the late 1970s, Ward Christensen invented the first public bulletin board system (BBS), which allowed people to post messages that others could read and respond to. One BBS, the WELL, gained tremendous popularity in the late 1980s and early 1990s as a well-known online community. Much of the early social psychology research done on online properties was focused on the WELL. Usenet, a system similar to BBSs, also found tremendous popularity in the 1980s as people posted articles and news to categories (called newsgroups). All of these social technologies predate the World Wide Web, which was invented by Sir Tim Berners-Lee in 1989.[11]

The web is incomparable. Now, nearly two decades after its invention, the world has completely and permanently changed. It's hard to imagine what life must have been like before we had web sites and applications.

Starting with the social software precursors mentioned above, the web has evolved toward more mature social software. What follows is a very abridged history of the web from a social software point of

---

9   For more insight into the reasons why people use MySpace, read Danah Boyd's: Identity Production in a Networked Culture: Why Youth Heart MySpace http://www.danah.org/papers/AAAS2006.html

10   http://en.wikipedia.org/wiki/Email

11   Super cool link: Tim Berners-Lee announcing the World Wide Web on Usenet: http://groups.google.com/group/alt.hypertext/msg/395f282a67a1916c

view. This is important because our audiences, except the youngest ones, have lived through and experienced this history and it shapes their expectations.

A One-Way Conversation (Read Only)

In 1995, back when Amazon was just a fledgling start-up, the web was quite a different place than it is now. It had just turned five years old. By one estimate it contained 18,000 web sites, total.[12] (Now there are hundreds of millions.) Most of those 18,000 web sites shared a common property: they were read-only. In other words, all you could do was read them. It was a one-way conversation. The information flowed from the person/organization who ran the site to the person viewing it. Sure, you could click on a link and be shown another page, but that was the extent of the interaction. Click, read, click, read. If you were lucky, the site might have listed a phone number that you could call.

That's not to say that people didn't use it socially. One person would write something on their web page, and a while later another would respond on their own web page. This made the conversation difficult, but possible. It's kind of like only being able to talk at your own house. When you want to say something, you and your friend go to your house. To get your friend's reply, you go to theirs.

A Two-Way Conversation (Read/Write)

Amazon and other pioneers then made a big leap forward: they figured out how to attach a database to the web site so they could store information in addition to simply displaying it. This capability, combined with cookies to save state information, as well as forms for inputting information, turned web sites into web applications. They were no longer read-only. They were read/write. Thus *two-way conversation* emerged on the web, a conversation between the person using the site and the person/organization who ran it.

A Many-Way Conversation (Social)

Next, as web applications became more sophisticated, designers tried new feature sets. As people got comfortable interacting with them, and as bandwidth increased and access became more pervasive, designers started to enable *many-to-many conversations*. Feature sets evolved based on which features survived in the new enviroment. Instead of just talking to the people who published a site, you could talk to all the other people who visited it as well.

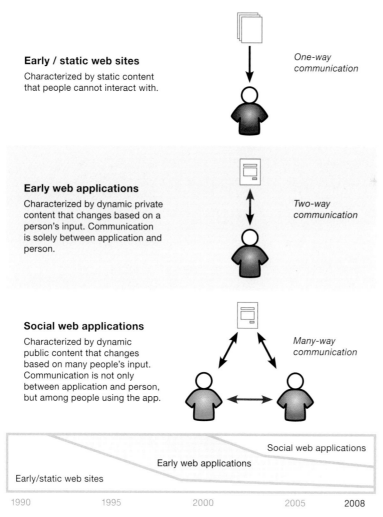

Early / static web sites
Characterized by static content that people cannot interact with.

One-way communication

Early web applications
Characterized by dynamic private content that changes based on a person's input. Communication is solely between application and person.

Two-way communication

Social web applications
Characterized by dynamic public content that changes based on many people's input. Communication is not only between application and person, but among people using the app.

Many-way communication

Social web applications

Early web applications

Early/static web sites

| 1990 | 1995 | 2000 | 2005 | **2008** |

Figure 1.2 The evolution of communication from one-way to many-way on the web.

As the power and reach of the web became evident in the last part of the 1990s, designers started to refashion bulletin board systems for the web, taking advantage of the knowledge gained from those earlier attempts. One casualty of this porting was that the original BBSs largely faded away.

These many-to-many conversations were a small step technologically but a huge step socially. When you go from talking to one party (the site owner) to talking to many parties (other visitors) you enable, for the first time, *group interaction*. Group interaction is what separates a web application from a *social* web application.

Another recent step that has brought this change into clearer focus is *ego-centric software*. The rise of social network sites like Friendster, MySpace, and Facebook has put the person at the center of the software. While there has always been talk about *community* on the web, web software makes a much deeper set of social interactions available to us. You can friend people. You can follow them. You can even send people a kiss.

The biggest web properties are social

Social web applications are now everywhere. Consider the following list of names you know and love, all of which are in the top 30 most-trafficked web properties in the U.S.:[13]

▶ YouTube grew faster than any web app in history as **millions of people uploaded homemade videos**

▶ Wikipedia is a **collaborative encyclopedia** written by tens of thousands of contributors around the world

▶ MySpace is by far **the most visited social network property**, with 65 million people a month visiting in December 2007[14]

▶ eBay is an amazing ecosystem where **perfect strangers exchange billions of dollars** a year in auctions without meeting face-to-face

▶ The photo sharing site Flickr allows millions of people to **share photos** with friends and loved ones

▶ Craigslist provides a simple interface where people can interact easily and do things, such as post **classifieds**, that they used to do in newspapers

---

13 According to Alexa, a useful tool for finding trends (but like all traffic measurement sites, any specific numbers from the site should be taken with a grain of salt).

14 http://siteanalytics.compete.com/myspace.com?metric=uv

▶ Facebook started on the Harvard campus by emulating an actual book handed out to freshmen (The Facebook) and grew into a behemoth of **social networking**

▶ IMDb aggregates the **movie ratings** of thousands of people to provide a helpful answer to the question, should I see this movie?

▶ Thousands of people on Digg, a social news site, **submit and rate stories** in an attempt to make it to the home page

▶ Google Search works by placing relevance on the **collective linking behavior** of the entire population on the web

▶ Yahoo's web-based Mail application is used by **hundreds of millions of people**

But those are just the biggest ones. Lots and lots of smaller social web applications are sprouting up as people get more comfortable with the idea of interacting socially. Here are some interesting ones:

▶ **Sermo.** A social network site that connects professional doctors in order to speed up information sharing and dissemination

▶ **PatientsLikeMe.** A social network site that provides support for people living with HIV, ALS, and others

▶ **Kiva.** A social network site that lets people in developed countries loan money to entrepreneurs in the developing world

▶ **Nike+.** An app for runners who can upload their personal exercise information and share with others

▶ **LibraryThing.** An app that allows you to upload and share your personal library and book ratings with others

▶ **RateMyProfessors.** A hilarious site that allows students to rate professors in a public forum for all to see

The Fastest Growing Web Properties Are Social

Social web applications are the fastest growing properties on the web. It's no wonder. Good social sites have social features that enable them to be shared easily. Their entire purpose is to connect people, and when they do that efficiently, they grow very quickly as a result.

YouTube, for example, streams over 100 million videos *per day*. One of its co-founders, Jawed Karim, notes very few people dispute that YouTube is the fastest growing web site in Internet history.[15]

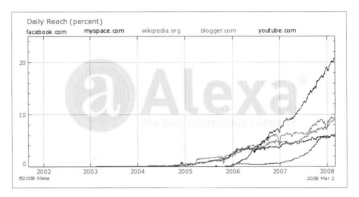

Figure 1.3 Social sites/applications/platforms are the fastest growing properties on the web.

Where Do You Spend Your Time?

Here's an amazing statistic:

In August 2007, over ten percent of the time Americans spent online was on a single social web app: MySpace.com.

With all the choices we have for where to spend our time, nearly twelve percent of all people's time is spent on a single site! In addition, a mere twenty web domains account for thirty-nine percent of our time online. Many of them are social web applications.

These numbers are startling for several reasons.

We are deeply attached. The average time per visit on MySpace is the length of a sitcom: twenty-six minutes.[16] And, since many people visit MySpace, Facebook, and other social network sites at least once per day, this lengthy stay is habitual. In other words, the social web is becoming a way of life.

We follow our friends. One of the more egalitarian promises of the web is that "every web site is equal." Any given site has just as much opportunity as the next one. But these numbers show that while this may be true in principle, in practice people strongly congregate where their social circles and their friends are.

15 http://www.youtube.com/watch?v=nssfmTo7SZg

16 http://blog.compete.com/2007/09/11/facebook-third-biggest-site-page-views-myspace-down/

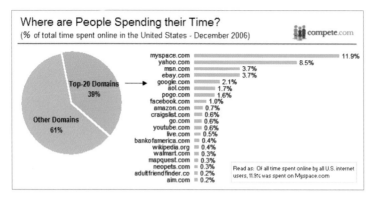

Figure 1.4 This graphic from Compete, an analytics company, shows how mad people are about MySpace. 11.9% of all online time in the U.S.? That's insane!

Blogs!

In addition to the big name sites above, there are an estimated 100 million blogs on the web. According to the blog-tracking site Technorati, in March 2007 there were approximately 70 million blogs, with 120,000 blogs being added every day![17] By the time this book is published, the number of blogs on the web will be over 100 million.

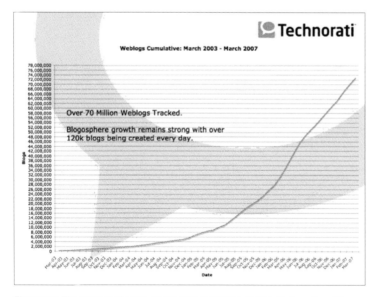

Figure 1.5 The number of blogs on the web is growing at an amazing rate, with no signs of stopping.

---

17 http://technorati.com/weblog/2007/04/328.html

Conclusion

Less Than 20% So Far

The growth of the social web is mind-boggling. Even more remarkable, however, is that this *growth is unlikely to slow down anytime soon.* According to InternetWorldStats, which aggregates statistics from sources like Nielsen/NetRatings:

Only 1.2 of the 6.5 billion people on Earth use the Internet. That's less than 20%.[18]

Despite the rich history of social software and the rich interactions happening already on sites like Amazon, we are still only at the beginning of the social web. As more and more people from around the world get access to the Internet and grow comfortable interacting socially online, we'll see a continued growth and maturation of social web applications. The successes of the moment (the Amazons, MySpaces, and Facebooks) will grow and change, and new applications will come to join them or take their place. That kids tend to intuitively grasp and embrace the social nature of the experience is a strong predictor of this future.

---

18 http://www.internetworldstats.com/stats.htm

A Framework for Social Web Design

The AOF method for making early and crucial design decisions

"It is easy in the world to live after the world's opinion; it is easy in solitude to live after our own; but the great man is he who in the midst of the crowd keeps with perfect sweetness the independence of solitude."

—Ralph Waldo Emerson

If there is one disease that affects nearly all design projects, it's *feature creep*. It is the deadly affliction in which design teams gradually add feature after feature, like straws on a camel's back, until they ultimately overload their interface and make the software difficult to use.

Feature creep happens when there is a lack of sustained focus on what's most important. Instead of deciding on a few core features to support, the team ends up trying to support too many. The software inevitably becomes harder to use, as features compete with each other within the interface.

To prevent feature creep, designers need to answer several questions early on in the design process. What is the primary activity our software is supporting? What features do we need to effectively support that activity? And, perhaps most importantly, what features can we leave out?

A lack of design focus can result from factors that seem, at first glance, out of the designer's control:

▶ **Competing interests**. Is marketing pushing one way, engineering another, and management yet another? When each part of a machine is geared to moving in its own direction, it hinders coordinated effort toward a common goal.

▶ **Political infighting**. Is arguing and disagreement stalling progress? Do team members disagree on major issues and refuse to budge? Do personalities clash?

▶ **Lack of audience clarity**. Do you know who to design for? Are you talking with them to find out exactly what their problems are?

▶ **Fuzzy strategy**. Does the strategic plan sound more like buzzword bingo? If you substituted someone else's strategy, would it change the way you do things?

▶ **No vision for success**. Do you know what success looks like? What has to happen to make you successful?

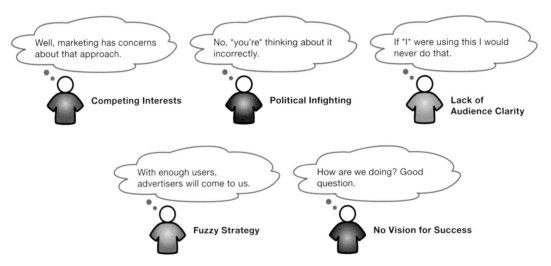

Figure 2.1 The issues that plague design teams come in many forms. A design framework can help focus a team on what's most important.

These issues constantly plague design teams. They serve to shift focus away from the design problem and cause frustration. Worst of all, they prevent designers from doing their best work.

A Prioritization Scheme

What design teams need is a way to prioritize and assess the value of proposed features. They need to know if a feature is worth the time and energy to implement and support. A prioritization scheme would help address the questions:

- ▶ Where should our design team focus its time and energy?
- ▶ What features should we consider adding? Improving? Removing?
- ▶ Will this feature set support our overall strategy?
- ▶ How do we get away from politics and competing interests and onto questions about the design itself?

The AOF Method

This chapter describes a simple prioritization scheme for designing social web applications that I call the *AOF Method*. AOF stands for **A**ctivities, **O**bjects, and **F**eatures.

The AOF Method is made up of three general steps.

1. **Focus on the primary Activity**. The first question you must answer (and always abide by while designing) is: *What is your audience doing?*

2. **Identify your social Objects**. Once you've got the activity down, you have to identify the objects that people interact with while doing that activity.

3. **Choose your core Feature set**. From the activity and objects you can derive a core feature set, answering the question: *What are the actions people perform on the objects, and which are important enough to support in the web application?*

Focus on the Primary Activity

As a designer, it has been drilled into your head to "know your users." This sounds like great advice: pay attention to the people you're designing for. But when we actually start to do that, it becomes pretty clear that the number of things we *could* pay attention to is never-ending. If we were to actually know our users in the true sense of that phrase, we would have to follow them home, stay overnight at their house, and hang out with them on the weekend.

Del.icio.us Lesson: Personal Value Precedes Network Value

One of the earliest lessons I learned in designing for the social web was that personal value must precede network value.

What do I mean by this? We live in a networked world, with our software connected to the web for increasingly long periods of time. We can collaborate and share information in amazing new ways, ways that weren't possible even five years ago. With this new ability comes an excitement about the social value of what we're building. Network value is new and exciting.

In our excitement over new ways to connect, we must not forget that all software begins by providing personal value to the individual.

The social bookmarking tool Del.icio.us was the first site to implement the feature that has come to be known as tagging. With tagging, people add words or phrases (tags) to bookmarks, allowing them to easily refind bookmarks later. Tagging items allows the site to do really interesting things, like aggregate everyone's tags to surface what tags are most popular, as well as see what items are being bookmarked most often.

Early on in the history of Del.icio.us, much was made of the social value of tagging. I was swept up in the excitement, wondering how this new tagging thing would change the world. But, as Del.icio.us' founder Joshua Schachter repeatedly pointed out, the major value of the site was "memory first, discovery second." The personal value of saving stuff for later comes before any social value of discovery the site might provide. Without support for the activity of bookmarking, all of that interesting social stuff doesn't exist.[1]

---

1 http://beth.typepad.com/beths_blog/2005/10/joshua_schachte.html

More important than knowing all about the *people* we design for, we should have a deep understanding of the specific *activity* we're supporting with our design. We should know all the steps taken in performing the activity, the decisions people need to make at each step, the influencing factors in those decisions, and what types of roles people are in when making them.[2] The time people spend using our design is the time they are doing some well-defined activity. The rest of their time on Earth, while interesting, doesn't affect our design very much.

For example, imagine we're designing software for photographers. What is helpful from a design standpoint are the similarities in what photographers do, not what makes them unique human beings. Many digital photographers want to upload and share their pictures immediately upon shooting. While they may each be shooting different subjects in different contexts, the activity of uploading and sharing is remarkably similar for each of them.

Thus the most important question we can ask is not "who is using your software?" but "what are people using your software doing?"

Only One Activity is Primary

Think about the software applications you use daily, the ones you rely on most. The most successful ones are focused applications that support one specific activity. Right?

Chances are you use email, chat, a word processor, a calendar, music player, photo editor, a spreadsheet, or some combination of those. You probably also use a web browser a lot. When you do go online, you probably encounter web applications supporting specific activities like banking, shopping, or managing your photos.

Simply put:

The applications people find most compelling allow them to excel at a single activity.

Consider the immensely popular site Flickr, which is focused on the activity of photo sharing. In personal terms, Flickr enables you to upload photos to share with family and friends. The designers at Flickr have added lots of features over the years, but they continue to focus on the same primary activity of photo sharing.

---

2   Don Norman has advocated for activity-centered design, even suggesting that human-centered design is harmful: http://www.jnd.org/dn.mss/humancentered_design.html

Another well-loved site is Etsy, which focuses on the activity of buying and selling homemade goods. Created as an antidote to eBay, the designers of Etsy focused on cultivating real relationships with the people who make the goods. All of the site's features revolve around that idea.

The more that sites like Flickr and Etsy focus on their primary activity, the more people seem to like them.

Kathy Sierra talks about this as the "I Rule" effect. The "I Rule" effect is when people start ignoring the software they're using and start to feel like an expert in what the software enables. You start to get a feeling like "I Rule!"

By focusing your software on a single activity, you make it much easier for the "I Rule" effect to happen. When your software is good at supporting its primary activity, like Flickr and Etsy are, then the person using it starts to feel great, not about your software, but about themselves. In Kathy's parlance, they become passionate users.

Identifying the Primary Activity

Unfortunately, identifying your primary activity isn't always easy. Try to answer this question:

What do people have to do in order for us to be successful?

If we were Amazon, we might answer: "purchasing goods." If we were Netflix, we might answer: "choosing movies to watch." If we were YouTube, we might answer: "uploading videos." These are the things that have to happen for these services to continue to be successful. But they are far from all that happens on these sites. They are critical tasks that make possible the larger activity. On Amazon, that larger activity is shopping. On Netflix, it's renting movies. On YouTube, it's sharing videos.

Goals, Activities, and Tasks

It is helpful to distinguish between goals, activities, and tasks. Goals are end conditions people are striving for. Activities are the set of tasks people do to achieve their goals.

Many times we focus too much on tasks instead of the larger activity. Instead of focusing on the task of "purchasing goods," it is more beneficial for design purposes to focus on the activity of shopping, as it better describes what's really going on.

This table distinguishes between goals, activities, and tasks:

Service	Goals	Activities	Tasks
Amazon	Procuring basic goods	Shopping	Adding to shopping cart, performing a product search, comparing products
Netflix	Entertainment	Renting movies	Rating movies, adding a movie to the queue, discussing movies with our partner
Monster	Making money	Finding a job	Searching for a job, sending a resume
Basecamp	Getting work done on time	Managing a project	Adding milestones, delegating tasks to others
Menuism	Eating well	Finding great places to eat	Rating and reviewing restaurants, reading others' reviews, making reservations, choosing a place to eat
Flickr	Staying up-to-date with family	Sharing photos	Uploading a picture, sending a URL via email to our mother

Thinking on the level of activities allows us focus on both the details of tasks as well as the overall goals of the people who use our software. Activities also allow us to take into consideration the social interactions we participate in when we solve problems, whether getting recommendations from trusted people or asking perfect strangers what they would do.

A few important points about activities:

Activities are important because they reveal the process. Activities allow us to discover the steps people take toward reaching their goals. People go through a series of tasks, and while doing so they rely on others for help. By looking at this on the activity level, we recognize all of these important pieces.

Many activities are about *managing* information. This is no accident, as many activities are inherently disorganized. If activities weren't messy, we might not need software to help us! People use software increasingly to manage activities.

Describe the activity in terms of the people you design for. Try not to describe the activity in terms of you, the designer. The activity is not "giving us money" or "using our stuff." These are simply byproducts (hopefully) of the activity itself.

Research Methods

Many research methods help us discover the details we need to know about activities. Most likely, design teams will have different ways of conducting research.

The important thing about research is that you get over any initial assumptions about the activity, which will be too broad. The following research methods are ways to get more insight into the activities you're designing for:

- ▶ **Interviews.** Interviews are powerful yet simple ways to get an insight into how people perform activities. When performing interviews, focus on what people do, not their opinions about what they do.

- ▶ **Usability testing.** You can set up usability tests in which you observe people using either competing software or an existing version of your software. This will give you insight into how people currently perform the activity and what parts of that activity aren't well-supported.

- ▶ **On-site observation.** Going to where the work you're supporting is actually done is a great way to dive into the details of the activity. This is called "contextual research," and it means that you do research in the context of work.

- ▶ **Observing yourself.** Observing yourself doing an activity can give you unique insight into the details of it. However, people are notoriously bad at observing themselves objectively, so it's best to combine any self-observation with observation of others.

- ▶ **Listening to people.** With features like product message boards, phone line support, and simple feedback forms, you can gain tremendous insight into the activity you're supporting.

The purpose of all of these research methods is to find out what is happening, why it is happening, and who it is happening among.[3]

After you do the research digging into the details of the activity you're supporting, you can inform future design more confidently. Don't be afraid to change your notions based on research! The key to any research effort is to observe and learn. As long as you are learning from real observations, you'll be ahead of the game.

---

3   A great resource on research methods is the book *Contextual Design* by Hugh Beyer and Karen Holtzblatt

Exercise: Researching the Activity of Shopping

Let's illustrate the value of research by doing an exercise. Let's imagine that you're building software that is going to support the primary activity of shopping. So start by writing down a description of the steps involved in shopping. Try to answer the question: what happens when someone shops? Don't read further until you have your list.

Actually make the list now.

A Normal View of Shopping

In describing the activity of shopping, most people will list four or five steps. Here is a list that I came up with off the top of my head. Let's call it the "normal" view of shopping.

- Recognize a need
- Consider the different choices of product that fulfills the need
- Choose a product
- Optionally, shop around for the best price
- Purchase the product

Your list will be slightly different, of course. But something like this is a basic shopping framework that most of us would come up with. Since most of us don't think about the activity of shopping in great detail, the steps we describe are high-level.

An Ethnographic View of Shopping

Ethnographers are people who study human activity. They know that you can't trust what people say, you have to observe what they do. They do *fieldwork* to understand what it is that people really do.

An ethnographer goes out into the wild and reports back. Here is what they might report when they observe someone shopping:

> We studied a woman (Betsy) who had several talks with her husband about upgrading their TV service to HD. He was all for it, but she was skeptical. Their conversations happened over the span of several months. She then heard about an HD TV from a close friend who had nothing but positive things to say. She started to seriously consider buying one, thinking that in addition to her husband's sports, an HD TV sounded like a better way to watch the nature shows that her children loved. She thought the product might be useful to her and her family. Betsy then decided that the family's 18-year-old TV had had enough. She and her husband made the decision to replace their aging TV with one of the HD TVs they heard about.

The ethnographer might ask who Betsy heard about the TV from. It was Betsy's friend Rachel, who recommended the 40" Sony HD TV she recently bought.

> While Betsy's husband is gung-ho, Betsy is the financial organizer of the household. Therefore, she does much of the research on projects like this. She starts doing research on this particular product, to find out more about it and see if it might fit their needs and desires. Part of her research is going online and reading about it. She goes to Amazon.com, BestBuy.com, and Sears.com. She finds out that there are more screen sizes, qualities, and price ranges than she had expected. She makes a list of items that seem comparable. She is quite confused by all the choices. This is a big hurdle for her.

> Another part of her research is talking to her close friends and other people she knows to have HD TVs, to see if they are familiar with the one she is considering. She trusts Rachel, but Rachel tends to recommend everything she has. Betsy wants second opinions. Have her other friends had good or bad experiences? Would they recommend the same TV? What other issues are there to consider? What should she watch out for? Are there alternative brands that she should look at?

> One of Betsy's other friends then tells her that buying the TV is only half of the issue. The other half is getting all the gear and cables to hook it up. Rachel hadn't mentioned these issues. Betsy is quite discouraged at this point. The old TV was so simple: you just plug it in and it works.

> At this point Betsy is in full research mode, with a lot of technical information swimming about in her head that wasn't there a week or two ago.

> Betsy and her husband think that the 40" is perfect for their needs and they don't want to buy a smaller one at this time. They consider if a particular HD TV fits within their budget. They decide that it's more than they want to pay, so they'll wait to see if it goes on sale.

> The family waits for a couple of weeks and then receives a coupon from Sears in the mail. They would rather pick it up than have to pay the shipping costs. They go to a store to purchase it.

Sweat the Details

Note the extreme difference in detail between the two views. The first view imagines a five-step, generic activity called shopping. The second view is a whirlwind of indecision, still *called* shopping, but more like a large project to find a TV that works well for the family. And, also note that this second view is only one example of shopping. Each shopping experience has the potential to have this much detail!

This second view is what most activities are like: longer than we think, messier than we think, and with much more detail than we realize. While not all of these details will translate directly to design, many will.

This is the value of real research into activities. It uncovers those things we just don't think of, but are all familiar with.

The Forgotten Element: Social Interaction

As the shopping example showed, people rarely make a decision without involving others in some way. Though most activities are social, much of the software designed today doesn't take advantage of the social interaction of the people who use it. This results from thinking about activities in over-simplistic ways, like we did in the earlier view of the shopping activity. What actually happens in activities is always much more complex than our conception of it.

Identify Your Social Objects

Once you start describing activities, you'll be struck by how big a role objects play in them. For example, in our table above each activity we mentioned had an associated object: movies, restaurants, projects, jobs, photos. A huge part of our activity is managing these objects and the social interactions that happen around them.

Social objects, as we may call the objects that mediate social activities, are often overlooked in the excitement about social software, in particular, social networking sites like MySpace and Facebook. Jyri Engeström, the founder of the social messaging software Jaiku, laments that too much focus in social design is on networking, and not the ever-present social objects that connect us all together:

> The term "social networking" makes little sense if we leave out the objects that mediate the ties between people. Think about the object as the reason why people affiliate with each specific other and not just anyone. For instance, if the object is a job, it will connect me to one set of people whereas a date will link me to a radically different group. This is common sense but unfortunately it's not included in the image of the network diagram that most people imagine when they hear the term "social network." The fallacy is to think that social networks are just made up of people.[4]

Discovering and modeling these social objects, and our interactions in and around them, is a major part in social design.

---

4   Please read Jyri's now classic post on object-centered sociality: http://www.zengestrom.com/blog/2005/04/why_some_social.html

Real-life Artifacts

Sometimes, you can even model real-life artifacts as objects in your design. Here are three that have replicated a physical object in software:

- ▸ **Facebook**. The Facebook is an actual book given out to Harvard students containing pictures and bios of all incoming freshmen, so they can enjoy finding out about their new classmates.

- ▸ **Amazon's Wish List**. Amazon's wish list is modeled after actual wish lists that people make and share with others.

- ▸ **Remember the Milk**. Remember the Milk is a list management tool that models the lists we make as we head out to do some shopping or roll up our sleeves to begin our chores.

Funky Objects

Social objects within your web application don't have to be exact representations of physical objects (like videos, photos, or dogs). They can be abstract.

For example, jobs and dates—the two objects Engeström mentions—are not physical in the sense that a table is, yet we easily deal with them on

Proven Success of Social Objects

The most successful web applications are built around social objects. Consider the following list of services. All the interactions on these sites happen in and around very specific social objects:

Flickr—Photos	**Del.icio.us**—Bookmarks	**Blogger**—Blogs
Amazon—Products (e.g. books)	**eBay**—Auction items	**Monster**—Jobs
YouTube—Videos	**Craigslist**—Classifieds	**Netflix**—Movies
Upcoming—Events	**Last.fm**—Music	**Slideshare**—Presentations
Twitter—Messages	**Digg**—News stories	**Wikipedia**—Encyclopedia entries
	Dogster—Dogs	

As we can see, social objects are really the starting point of a lot of social web applications. They are the objects around which many of our activities revolve. Identifying these objects is crucial to designing for them.

a daily basis. *Projects* and *events* are also abstract, but we organize our activities around them effortlessly.

What's important is not that you have a single, physical object to focus on, but that you focus on a social object in the same way the people who use your software do. If people are organizing around funky objects like projects, then that's an object you can design for.

Give the Social Objects a URL

To demonstrate the proven success of social objects earlier in this chapter, I listed a number of services that contain unique objects. There are distinct advantages to giving an object a URL:

▸ URLs make objects sharable

▸ URLs make objects easier to find and re-find

▸ URLs allow people to link to the object directly

▸ Search engines like URLs

Flickr's URLization of Photos

The success of the photo-sharing site Flickr is tied closely with their decision to give photos a unique URL. Team member Eric Costello describes their transition from allowing people to share photos over chat to allowing people to archive photos at a URL.

Before URLs:

> When we first launched Flickr, it was a Flash application that was mainly just a chat environment with real-time photo sharing. So it was quite limited in what you could do.
>
> It wasn't a photo sharing site, so much as it was a place where you could go to chat and talk about photos. But none of that activity was stored in any asynchronous way.

After URLs:

> As we started adding features to the site itself, like pages that hosted the photos so that people could visit them at a unique URL, we had a lot more success with that. People responded to it, and the site began to grow.[5]

---

5   http://adaptivepath.com/ideas/essays/archives/000519.php

So once Flickr identified photos as their object and gave them a unique URL, their service started taking off. This makes sense: objects are unique, and giving them a unique URL allows people to treat them like freestanding objects. Once photos had a unique URL, they became addressable by anyone and everyone.

Choose a Core Feature Set

After identifying the primary activity and the objects people interact with, you're ready to start creating your core feature set. Your core feature set is the set of possible actions that people can do in your application. They define what activity goes on, the possible interactions between people, what can and—sometimes just as importantly—cannot occur. Choosing features is one of the most important steps in defining what a web site is going to be.

Finding Your Verbs

In the beginning of this chapter we mentioned feature creep, the disease that afflicts so many design projects. So how do you avoid feature creep when creating and adding features? Start with your objects, your *nouns*. Observe all the *actions* people do with/perform on those objects, and those are possible features for your application.

Jyri Engeström calls this step "finding your verbs." Given a noun, what actions are associated? The answer, as our high school English teachers would point out, is indeed a list of verbs.

Here are some examples of finding verbs:

Nouns (objects)	Verbs (actions)
Videos	play, stop, edit, store, upload, share, comment on, embed in blog
Articles	read, archive for later, quote, link to, share, comment on, annotate
Photos	store, view, add to favorites, digitally edit, link to, make prints, share, comment on, embed in blogs, tag
Books	read, add to cart, purchase, add to wish list, share, add to wedding registry, comment on, rate, tag, discuss, review

Many of these verbs translate *directly* into features. If you're building a video site, for example, you'll likely have features to upload a video, play the video, and share the video. This simple step is where the most valuable features come from!

Also, notice that the verbs are both personal *and* social. This is to be expected, as we interact with objects both on a personal level and a social level.

Figure 2.2 The entire YouTube interface is made up of objects (nouns) and the actions you can perform on them (verbs). If you take the nouns and verbs off the page, there is very little, if anything, left.

Collections of Objects as Features

Pay attention to any collections of objects. They can often become valuable features. One important collection is lists. Are people making lists? What of? How are they organizing and managing information? Here are some common ways that people collect things:

- Wish lists
- Shopping carts
- Favorites
- Shared items
- My stuff (restaurants, reviews, bookmarks, etc.)
- Friend's stuff
- Projects

Once you have an idea of the collections that people make, give them ways to manage the collection. What actions (verbs) do they perform on the collection? This will probably mean providing people with ways to add, edit, and delete items from the collection, and perhaps even treating the collection as an object itself, with features such as sharing and a permalink.

Amazon's Social Features

Let's explore the social features on the Amazon site in light of the AOF method. As you can see, Amazon has a tremendous number of social features to help make shopping easier.

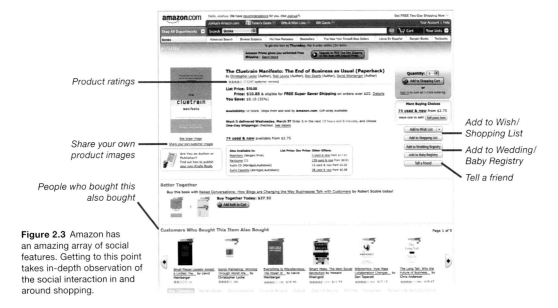

Product ratings

Share your own product images

People who bought this also bought

Add to Wish/ Shopping List

Add to Wedding/ Baby Registry

Tell a friend

Figure 2.3 Amazon has an amazing array of social features. Getting to this point takes in-depth observation of the social interaction in and around shopping.

Amazon sales rank

Popular in these categories

Update Product Info

Give feedback on images

What do customers ultimately
buy after viewing this item?

Tag this item

Help others find this item

Sell yours here

Rate this item to improve your
recommendations

Customer Reviews

Was this review helpful to you?

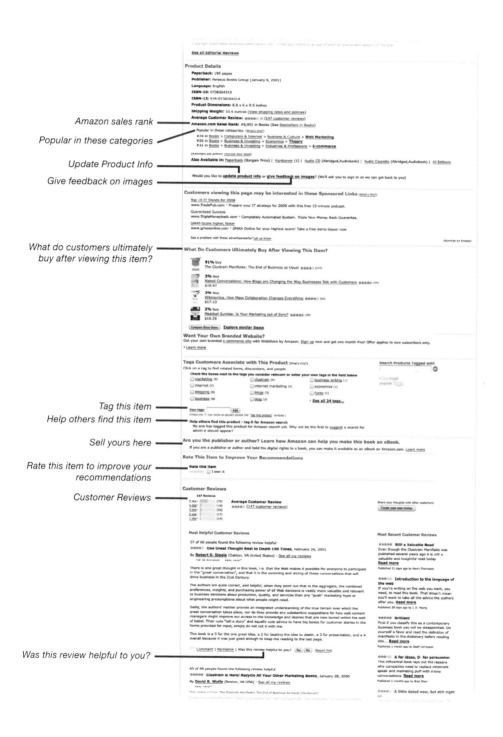

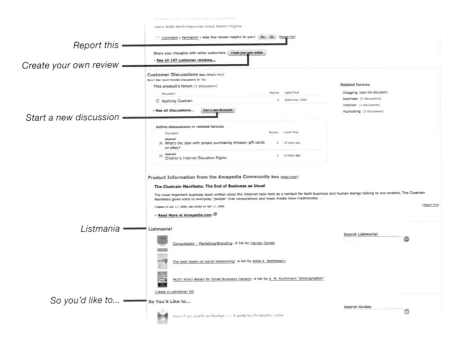

Report this

Create your own review

Start a new discussion

Listmania

So you'd like to...

We can see that most of the actions support the most important object, the product. Amazon has focused most of their time and energy there. But they have also identified other important objects central to the activity of shopping, and include features to support those.

If we were designing with a common-sense notion of shopping, without doing any research, we would design a very different web site than we would with an ethnographer's detailed study in our hands. It would be difficult to come up with the social features at Amazon from team meetings and common sense. It is only by paying close attention to how people shop, the reasons why they make lists, their heavy reliance on customer reviews, and their tendency to look at sales numbers, that we would be able to come up with these interface features. *Sweat the details!*

Once you start thinking about features as actions to be done on objects, it becomes clear how the most successful services figure out which features to add. They simply answer the question: *What are people doing with the objects?*

The table that follows looks at Amazon's core features in this way.

Objects	Social Features (actions)
Products	Rate product
	Tag product
	Review product
	Customers who bought this also bought
	Submit a product manual
	Tell a friend
	Share product images
	Amazon sales rank
	Add to cart
Wish list	Add items
	Create new list
	Share list
	Make public/private
	Sort list
Customer reviews	Add review
	Comment on review
	Was this review helpful?
	Sort reviews

Keeping a Check on Features

As we have noted, features can get out of hand quickly. Here are a few guidelines to keep in mind when designing that help you deal with features reasonably.

Each Feature Means More Complexity

There is no way around it: each feature in your web site adds complexity. The process of introducing it, shifting other things around, re-prioritizing things is complex. When this is done well, people adapt quickly. When this is done poorly, the interface becomes more complex and you start hearing complaints.

Just Say No

One way to counteract adding too many features is to simply say "No" to them. Accept only the most important features, and keep the others on the back burner until they are truly necessary.

There is a great story about the building of iTunes that applies here. Steve Jobs was talking to music industry people about the direction the software was going. They had all sorts of ideas for what the software could possibly do. After a while Steve got tired of the queries, and said:

> I know you have a thousand ideas for all the cool features iTunes *could* have. So do we. But we don't want a thousand features. That would be ugly. Innovation is not about saying yes to everything. It's about saying NO to all but the most crucial features.[6]

Don't Copy Features!!!

One client I worked with would copy features that looked useful from their competitors. They said they didn't have time to fully research features themselves. Later, I ended up speaking with someone from the design team of that competitor, and it turns out they did the same thing! They simply copied their features from somewhere else!

The Emerson quote at the beginning of this chapter is relevant here. It's easy to simply copy features when everyone is looking at you. Your site looks like everyone else's and people assume you know what you're doing. It's also easy to go your own way when nobody is looking at you. But it is the most difficult (yet most successful) when you can do your own research and innovate in the face of scrutiny. That's why the best designs stand out...because they go their own way.

Conclusion

At some point all design teams struggle with a lack of focus. There are many reasons why. It helps to have a prioritization scheme like the Activities, Objects, Features method (AOF) to keep things focused. By keeping an eye on the primary activity and the objects related to it, designers can come up with a robust feature set that really does support what people are trying to do.

But as exciting as it is to get features in place, it is only the beginning of the battle in creating a social web site. You still have to motivate people to actually use the features you've created! That's what we cover in the rest of the book, focusing on the major hurdles of usage that affect all projects.

---

6   http://www.oreillynet.com/onlamp/blog/2004/08/say_no_by_default.html

Authentic Conversations

Why having authentic conversations is the most important thing you can do for your social web site

"The long silence—the industrial interruption of the human conversation—is coming to an end. On the Internet, markets are getting more connected and more powerfully vocal every day. These markets want to talk, just as they did for the thousands of years that passed before market became a verb with us as its object."

—THE CLUETRAIN MANIFESTO

On June 21, 2005, noted media industry veteran Jeff Jarvis was having a bad time with his Dell laptop. He was having an even worse time with the service he was receiving from the computer company. He had bought an expensive warranty that he felt Dell wasn't honoring, and he was getting the runaround on the phone. Jeff decided to vent his frustrations by posting them on his blog[1] for all to see:

June 21, 2005

Dell lies. Dell ▬▬

Dell lies. Dell ▬▬

: I just got a new Dell laptop and paid a fortune for the four-year, in-home service.

The machine is a lemon and the service is a lie.

I'm having all kinds of trouble with the hardware: overheats, network doesn't work, maxes out on CPU usage. It's a lemon.

But what really irks me is that they say if they sent someone to my home -- which I paid for -- he wouldn't have the parts, so I might as well just send the machine in and lose it for 7-10 days -- plus the time going through this crap. So I have this new machine and paid for them to ▬▬ FIX IT IN MY HOUSE and they don't and I lose it for two weeks.

DELL ▬▬. DELL LIES. Put that in your Google and smoke it, Dell.

Posted by jarvis at 09:48 PM | Comments (253)

Figure 3.1 The original post from Jeff Jarvis that started the Dell Hell series on his blog.

Ten years ago, the only way this information would have been made public is through whatever effort Jeff could make to tell his friends or perhaps write a letter to the editor. Maybe a reporter would have picked it up and written a story about it. Either way, the audience who would have seen it would have been relatively small. But, in the age of blogging, Jeff's story was available for everyone to see, 24 hours a day, 365 days a year, right on Jeff's web site. Jeff called his situation "Dell Hell."

Over the following weeks, Jeff continued to be unhappy with the service from the company, and continued to post his frustrations on his blog. Pretty soon others had picked up on his plight and joined him in a chorus of hatred for Dell. Hundreds and hundreds of people left comments on his blog.

It turns out that Jeff's situation wasn't isolated. Many other people felt strongly that the company was providing poor service. In fact, some bloggers directed Jeff's attention to similar posts they had made in the months and years prior to his post about bad service from Dell.

---

1   http://www.buzzmachine.com/archives/2005_06_21.html#009911

At this point Dell—already aware of how upset people were with their service—had a choice. Would they engage with Jeff and other people who voiced their opinion, or would they leave it be and hope it went away?

Up until that point, Dell had a "look, don't touch" policy, observing stories like this from afar, but not responding in any way.[2] Would they change that policy in the face of mass public scrutiny?

Much to its own detriment, Dell continued its silence. The story of Dell Hell grew bigger. Dozens of blogs picked up on it, and news outlets too. The negative story about Dell's support spread far and wide.

The Growing Alienation

Dell is by no means alone in their disengagement. Our frustration with corporations is at an all-time high. The very companies we entrust with our business are ignoring us, even though we, the customers, are the reason for their success. And worst of all, we're so used to it that we seem to accept it as a matter of course. I was reminded of this the other day after spending forty minutes on hold with my web-hosting provider, and coming out of it not the least bit surprised. I realized with self-loathing that I accepted this as par for the course when dealing with companies. Did they not think my time was important? Did they care? If they cared, I had no evidence of it. And, as Jeff's situation made perfectly clear, countless people are experiencing this alienation every day.

Doc Searls, in *The Cluetrain Manifesto*, describes this alienation:

> In the twentieth century, the rise of mass communications media enhanced industry's ability to address even larger markets with no loss of shoe leather, and mass marketing truly came into its own. With larger markets came larger rewards, and larger rewards had to be protected. More bureaucracy, more hierarchy, and more command and control meant the customer who looked you in the eye was promptly escorted out of the building by security.[3]

---

2   http://www.buzzmachine.com/archives/2005_07_09.html#010024

3   http://www.cluetrain.com/book/markets.html

People Who Build Web Applications are Especially Vulnerable

If you're building a web application, you are especially vulnerable to this growing alienation, for several reasons:

▶ **No face-to-face contact.** It is unlikely that you will see any of the people who use your software face-to-face. Therefore, it is important to reach out and have conversations over social software. This kind of interaction is slightly harder because the nuance of interpersonal communication is lost.

▶ **Frustration is invisible.** Unless someone makes the effort to tell you when something goes wrong, you won't know when problems arise. They may languish in their own frustration until they give up or complain in some other way, like Jeff and others did on their blogs.

▶ **Support is part of the product.** To the people who use your software, there is little distinction between the application and the support you provide for it. Web-based software isn't so much a product as it is a service. The service—including the quality of support and other interactions—is the value you deliver, and thus quality customer relations are crucial.

What Could it Look Like?

Dell's choice to not engage Jeff in conversation was a poor one. It would have been a poor decision even if Jeff was not well known with a big audience. It was a poor decision simply because he was a customer *at all*. Every day, Dell was ignoring the frustration of the people who made and could continue to keep them successful.

But it doesn't have to be this way. Consider the reply on Christina Wodtke's blog[4] after she posted concerns about Plaxo's privacy policy concerning emailing contacts. (Plaxo is an online contact manager and Christina is the tech editor of this book.) The message left by Stacy Martin, the Privacy Officer at Plaxo, serves as a wonderful example of how you can engage with people, address their concerns, and make them feel heard.

---

4 Christina's blog can be found at http://www.eleganthack.com/blog

Notice that Stacy does several things well in this message. First, by using his real name and position at the company, he instantly establishes his credibility. Second, he addresses Christina's concerns directly, acknowledging (without actually knowing) that something wrong may have occurred. He asks Christina to contact him directly to address Christina's specific situation. He also explains Plaxo's general philosophy on sharing information, which informs others who read the blog that Plaxo is serious about privacy. He doesn't argue or get upset. He is authentic.

Plaxo with caution

I just reinstalled Plaxo, in order to get my address book back after my laptop died. I updated my business card. Little did I know, Plaxo emailed all my contacts. I was not warned, I was not told I should double check my spelling or information before sending it out... nope, Plaxo just took it upon itself to spam everyone with the new card. This program's bad UI choices has now endangered relationships. I am steaming mad, and cannot figure out how to counter this amazing faux pas of software, except to uninstall Plaxo and warn everyone else I can find not to use it.

update: Be sure to read the comments

Figure 3.2 Christina Wodtke posts about an issue she had with Plaxo, an online contact manager. Note that she updated the post to make sure that people read the comment from the Plaxo representative. Authentic conversations work like that.

My name is Stacy Martin and I am the Privacy Officer here at Plaxo responsible for addressing Privacy, Security, and Trust issues pertaining to the usage of Plaxo.

Plaxo does not email your contacts any information without the action and approval of the Plaxo member. Perhaps you can contact me directly so we can determine what may have occurred in your case.

To explain a bit of how Plaxo works: when a user first successfully installs Plaxo, the default action is to launch the Update Contacts Wizard.

This wizard walks the Plaxo member through 3 simple steps for sending an Update Request message. No Update Request message will be sent without the user first successfully completing the entire wizard process and approving the action.

As part of this process, the Plaxo member must select who they wish to send the Update Request to, what personalized message they wish to include within the Update Request message, and what information of their own they wish to attach to the message. After completing these steps, the Plaxo member is shown a summary of what action will be take and then they must approve and then confirm the action (two separate steps) before anything is executed. At any step in the process, the member can also choose to abort.

But if you believe that something else may have occurred in your case, please let me know so we can investigate and figure out what may have occurred.

On a related note, when you change your Plaxo card information, Plaxo will automatically update those other Plaxo member you have previously granted permission to your Plaxo card information. Plaxo will automatically update your entry within their address books, and send the Plaxo member an Alert email to inform them of the action. This is the fundamental syncronization service that Plaxo provides to keep friends, family and associates updated. Is is possible that some of your friends may also be Plaxo members and received this type of Plaxo Alert email?

Please let me know. My contact info is below.

Stacy Martin
Plaxo Privacy Officer
privacy @t plaxo.com

Figure 3.3 A wonderful example of how customer service on the web can work.

The Value of Authentic Conversation

What Dell should have done, of course, is simply have a conversation with Jeff and his readers, just like Stacy of Plaxo did with Christina. This would have been easy for Dell to do: the company has thousands of employees and a large marketing group. A single employee could have quelled this uprising by simply engaging in conversation.

But engaging in authentic conversations isn't just about quelling negative sentiment from frustrated customers. That frustration is simply a symptom of *not* engaging.

The long-term benefits of actively engaging—*happier people* and *better software*—vastly exceed the short-term pain from negative press.

Happier People

Having authentic conversations with the people who use your software is a win-win situation. It drives the following advantages:

- **Recognition that you care.** When you have authentic conversations with people, you show that you care about their situation. Whatever the reality, Dell's lack of outreach gave Jeff Jarvis the feeling that Dell didn't care. When you start having conversations with people, they'll give you the benefit of the doubt.

- **Awareness and interest.** You'll also gain awareness and interest in your software. This happens because people respond to *and act favorably toward* those who talk to them. This isn't supposed to be magic. It's a core principle of human communication. So as you pay attention to people and respond to their needs, they'll start paying more attention to you as well. The relationship thus grows stronger, benefitting both sides.

Unaware   *Awareness*   **Interested**

Figure 3.4 Getting people interested in your software doesn't happen overnight. It's more like an evolving relationship that relies on authentic conversation.

Better Software

The counter-intuitive part of having authentic conversations is how they can actually lead to better software. In other words, having authentic conversations actually helps you design!

▶ **Ear to the ground.** When you have conversations with people, you have a much better sense of what's going on and can react much more quickly should a problem arise.

▶ **More design data.** Having conversations allows you to gather much more information to inform your design. This will lower the cost of other research methods.

▶ **Passionate feedback.** Until you've met passionate users, it's hard to imagine how much feedback they'll gladly give you about your software. I remember the first time I encountered passionate users—it was a chore just to record all of their feedback.

▶ **Users as inventors.** Not only do people provide great feedback, but they also become co-inventors. Look no further than the open-source movement for passionate users who get involved in building the product itself.

The Trick of Authenticity

Client: *This sounds great! I can get awareness and interest, find out what people think, and get people connected to my company. Sign me up for this authentic conversation feature.*

Me: *Well… there is one more thing.*

Client: *What's that?*

Me: *You have to mean it.*

Customer Service is the New Marketing

Marketing, which is defined as "the action or business of promoting and selling of products or services"[5] becomes much easier when you focus on having authentic conversations with the people who use your software.

When you have authentic conversations with people, you learn enough to actually improve your product with them, freeing you from the need for the hard sell. No longer will you have to convince people your software is worth it, because by working with the very people you're selling to, you're guaranteeing a valuable product.

This kind of interaction has traditionally been thought of as customer service. Brad Burnham, a venture capitalist who invests in early-stage social software, learned this by observing the way Craigslist worked. He says "customer service is the new marketing":

> Customer service is the new marketing because you can realize the radical efficiencies of the web only by enlisting the users of the service as co-contributors. The best web services provide bandwidth, cpu, storage and a governance system and then their users create the service. This is certainly true of Craigslist but it is also true of more commercial implementations like YouTube, Flickr, and del.icio.us. So if your users are your co-contributors, your co-creators really, what does it mean to sell them?

> If you need to convince your contributors of the value of your service you have probably already lost. All of the web services I mentioned are free, so selling them doesn't make literal sense anyway. What you can do is serve them, and serving them is the best marketing you can do. Why, because only by serving them, can you learn what it is that would make the service more useful to them.[6]

For social software the most effective marketing plan includes:

1. Make the real commitment to authentic conversation
2. Get attention by focusing on a specific community
3. Keep attention and build trust by reacting positively to negative feedback

---

5   this definition is taken from the Dictionary on my Mac

6   Brad's entire post is valuable reading: http://www.unionsquareventures.com/2006/11/customer_servic.html

Make the Commitment to Authentic Conversation

Simply having a conversation doesn't necessarily create awareness, interest, or better software. Conversation—at least the act of initiating it—only amplifies the existing sentiment.

In other words, if you decide to have a conversation with people about your software and:

a. **Your service stinks:** the resulting conversation will be about how much it stinks.

b. **Your service is great:** the resulting conversation will be about how great it is.

Tip: It's better to think of technology like blogs, forums, and discussion boards as amplifying customer opinion rather than improving it.

No matter what technology you use, the point is to have real conversations with people. If you do start having conversations with your audience and it turns out that your product stinks, you then have two options. You can:

a. **Listen to the feedback** (positive or negative), engage with those people, and improve your product/service.

b. **Ignore the feedback**, keeping your product/service the same, and continue not improving.

Actually, there is a third choice. If you really don't want to succeed, you can disagree with the feedback.

Finally, if you take the first choice and choose to engage and improve, you will start to realize a positive vibe. People will start to recognize that you actually *care*. And since companies that care are so rare, your customers will go tell their friends about it. Then you'll have the buzz and demand!

Making this choice is making the *commitment to authentic conversation*. It is the best thing you can do for the long-term health of your software. It is the key to the kingdom, so to speak, because when you are having authentic conversations, you will find out everything you need to improve over time. Authentic conversations give you a chance to show you care.

Ten Steps to Authenticity

Nobody can force you to care. But assuming that you *do* care, there are some very concrete things to do that *show* you care.

1. **Don't wait for conversation: initiate it.** Yes, create a blog, or at least have some forum for discussion, and then create conversations. Ask people what is important to them. Ask them what they care about in relation to what you do.

2. **Publish the real story of your company/organization.** Tell people what you believe in, how you got to be where you are, where you hope to go. This will attract like-minded people.

3. **Publish your views on privacy and support.** Explain what type of relationship you want with people.

4. **Listen, internalize, and respond thoughtfully.** Don't disagree, work together. Make it obvious you're listening.

5. **Help people learn about your software at their own pace.** Provide different levels of learning material: tutorials, manuals, help documents.

6. **Make feedback a top priority.** Give people an easy way to shoot you an email. Have a prominent contact page on your site and have someone read the messages promptly.

7. **Form a partnership with your customers.** Work together to solve their problems. Don't just provide solutions they have to take or leave, give them options.

8. **Make authentic conversation a part of the culture.** Get everyone involved. Designers, developers, everyone. Give everybody the ability to reach out to customers. Make authentic conversations a mandate for all people who touch the software in any way.

9. **Anticipate and act on change.** Recognize that feedback is a natural part of design, and that people who are passionate about your products will naturally have more feedback. They care.

10. **Hire a community manager!** Even better, hire someone who is already a passionate member of the community.

The Importance of a Community Manager

The founder of Craigslist, Craig Newmark, thinks community management is so important that he does it himself. Of all the jobs a founder could possibly do to run the company, Newmark focuses on the one that seemingly anyone can do.

> I figure that reasonably good customer service is part of the social contract between producer and consumer. In general, if you're going to do something, you should follow through and not screw around. As a nerd, I have the tendency to take things pretty seriously, so if I commit to something, I try really hard to stay committed.
>
> This isn't altruism or social activism; it's just giving people a break. Pretty much all world religions tell us that one moral value is to help other people if you can. I feel that customer service, even when you get paid for it, is an expression of that value, an everyday form of compassion.[7]

It is easy to see from Craig's description how integral he thinks customer service is to the experience of people using the site.

While it's easy to think of customer service as "dealing with the public," Craig has a more optimistic view of the people he deals with:

> We've found people to be extremely trustworthy. People are overwhelmingly good and if you trust them and seriously engage and try your best to work with people, they'll work with you in return.... At Craigslist the company we just run the infrastructure and do customer service. People respond by doing things on the site and giving everyone else a break and that really works pretty well.[8]

What Community Managers Do

Why am I talking about community management in a design book?

Here's why: to the customer who is using your service, there is no difference between the software and support. When people use your software, when they're interacting with it, and they need help, they don't expect to get it from somewhere else. Since you, the designer, are planning the experience they're having, it's up to you to make it right.

---

7   http://www.techreview.com/Infotech/14678/

8   http://gelconference.com/06/craig.html

In some cases, the managers are the designers. The designers at 37signals describe their philosophy of feeling their customers' pain:

> At 37signals, all of our support emails are answered personally by the people who actually build the product. Why? First off, it provides better support for customers. They're getting a response straight from the brain of someone who built the app. Also, it keeps us in touch with the people who use our products and the problems they're encountering. When the're frustrated, we're frustrated. We can say, "I feel your pain" and actually mean it.[9]

Community managers are part of the business, they are not consultants or outside help. They need to have intimate ties with both designers and developers, so when a difficult situation arises, they can fully explain it to your customers.

Community Building isn't about Features

If there were one immutable law of social software, it would be this:

Technology cannot solve people problems.

No matter how great the technology you're using, it can't solve what are fundamentally human social problems. Garnering interest, getting people excited and talking about our software: the things we really want take real people making human-to-human contact. There is no way around it. So forget easy technological solutions. Technology might help you along the way, but it can't have conversations for you and it's no substitute for actual human interaction.

Take, for instance, the following list of ten ways to build community created by Heather Champ, community manager at Flickr. Notice that not one of the ways Flickr builds community is about a feature. She never even mentions them!

---

9   http://gettingreal.37signals.com/ch14_Feel_The_Pain.php

Ten Ways Flickr Builds Communities[10]

1. **Engage.** Don't just listen to your community

2. **Enforce.** Let the community help set standards and policies for appropriate behavior—then enforce them

3. **Take Responsibility.** Fess up immediately when you make mistakes

4. **Step Back.** Don't be afraid to step back and let your customers take over

5. **Give Freely.** Never underestimate the allure of a free T-shirt (or sticker, or button…)

6. **Be Patient.** Take knee-jerk reactions with a grain of salt

7. **Hire Fans.** Make sure your employees are as passionate about your product as your community's most die-hard fans

8. **Stay Calm.** Develop a thick skin

9. **Focus.** Be flexible but don't lose sight of your priorities

10. **Be Visible.** Stay human

Instead, Heather talks about human-to-human interaction: ways to take responsibility, ways to communicate how you want the community to act. That, not features, is what it takes to manage a community.

Get Attention by Focusing on a Specific Community

It's hard to imagine that many of the behemoth web sites and applications we deal with on a daily basis all started from nothing. Many of the sites share something similar and counter-intuitive, though. They grew large not by focusing on large audiences, but by focusing on small, specific communities and growing from there.

---

10 http://images.businessweek.com/ss/07/09/0914_flickr/index_01.htm

▸ **Facebook.** Facebook started in the concentrated microcosm of the Harvard University campus and then spread to other campuses

▸ **Amazon.** The sell-everything-under-the-sun Amazon started out by focusing principally on books

▸ **Flickr.** Flickr grew out of photo-sharing features created for an online game called Game Neverending

▸ **YouTube.** YouTube started as a simple tool for friends to share videos

▸ **Craigslist.** Craigslist started as an email list of San Francisco events for friends of its founder, Craig Newmark

Craig explains how he turned a small, focused list into the Craigslist of today by simply listening to customers:

> Craigslist was originally a very simple e-mail list for my friends, focusing on arts and technology events in San Francisco. People suggested doing more, like job and apartment listings, so I did that; then I got more feedback—so I did even more stuff. Today, Craigslist helps people in more than 100 cities in 24 countries with everyday needs, like finding a place to live or getting a job or selling furniture…. We have a pretty good culture of trust and goodwill.[11]

By focusing on a very small community, you can get valuable feedback that will help you when you want to focus on a larger community down the road.

If Possible, Build for Yourself

There's an interesting trend among successful web applications that isn't always apparent. Many successful apps are built by the same people who use them. In other words, designers and developers build for themselves.

There are lots of advantages to building for yourself:

▸ Less user research to do because you are the target user. Your use is user research.

▸ You're using it from day one. This means that you are dealing with the core issues each and every day.

▸ You're finding all the little nits, quirks, and hiccups that only real use finds. This is invaluable.

---

11 http://www.techreview.com/Infotech/14678/

But perhaps the biggest difference of building for yourself is passion. People who build for themselves are almost always more passionate than folks building for someone else.

Dan Cederholm, designer of the social wine application Corkd,[12] which allows people to share their wine experiences with others, nicely sums up the difference:

> There's a real difference between being a hired hand on a project for a specific amount of time and someone who has ownership as well as passion for what they're working on (ownership and passion can be exclusive as well, but combined, they pack quite a punch). The short-term, part-time attention of a freelance designer or developer can often lead to clunky, duct-taped solutions after the contract is over and the site is actually being used by real people. Cork'd has been the complete opposite situation, where we've been able to launch a product that would be considered "done" under most circumstances and then react to member feedback using the same attention to detail that went into the initial construction.[13]

Build Outwards

When you build for yourself, the next logical step is to have your friends try it out. This is not just for fun, though. This is the beginning of spreading the goodwill about your web application. So you'll want to not only seed your application to your long-time friends, but you'll want to identify people who would be very good people to know, get feedback from, and tell others.

Building outwards is much easier than releasing to the general public without a solid starting point. It's akin to planting a few small seedlings and focusing on them instead of scattering seeds on the ground and hoping some take root. Yes, you start off with a smaller area covered, but what is there is healthier and already alive. Its growing, while your far-flung seeds may or may not take.

Also, when the people helping you realize they're part of an early project, they're much more likely to support you. People root for underdogs. It's in our nature. They don't see it as trouble to use software that isn't perfect, in fact, they want to help make it perfect.

---

12 http://corkd.com

13 http://www.simplebits.com/notebook/2006/05/30/update2.html

Release Early, Release Often

Eric Raymond, in the classic open-source manifesto *The Cathedral and the Bazaar,* says that open-source succeeds in big part by adopting a strategy of "release early and often."[14]

This has several effects:

- ▸ Builds goodwill
- ▸ Shows people that you're there and improving
- ▸ Gets people coming back often
- ▸ Lets you fail fast

A major benefit of fast iteration is you also fail fast. Failing fast means you invest less time in the things that don't work. If you find what doesn't work quickly, then you quickly take action to turn it into something that does work.

Ironically, teams that fail fast improve faster than those who try to get everything right at every iteration. The reason is simple: Teams trying to get everything right fail as often as everyone else does. However, they struggle to pinpoint problems because they've changed so many things.

More Experimentation, Reduced Risk

The faster you fail, the more experimentation you can do. You can try out ideas that might not have a lot of support, but could be potential winners. The strategy of making many small changes instead of a few larger ones allows for an innovative environment, yet it also mitigates risk because you can evaluate which changes have what effect and can be confident in keeping only the positive ones.

Learn Quickly

We've all had the experience of sitting in meetings arguing about whether something will work. Usually, neither side has enough data to go on, and they end up going with their gut or with the loudest arguer, for better or worse. Fast iteration helps solve this problem by giving developers a platform on which they can test quickly and collect data about any outstanding questions, instead of resorting to opinion.

---

14 http://catb.org/~esr/writings/cathedral-bazaar/cathedral-bazaar/ar01s04.html

Provide Continuing Interest

In addition to improving your design, fast iterations may have a psychological effect on users. People who use your site with any frequency will notice the changes, and if the good ones stick, they'll appreciate your ongoing efforts to improve.

The best teams not only design the changes, but design the process for introducing the change. They experiment with methods to overcome people's natural resistance to change, providing migration paths and clear benefits for each improvement.

The Building of Gmail

Paul Buchheit describes the release early, release often evolution of Gmail:

> I wrote the first version of Gmail in one day. It was not very impressive. All I did was stuff my own email into the Google Groups (Usenet) indexing engine. I sent it out to a few people for feedback, and they said that it was somewhat useful, but it would be better if it searched over their email instead of mine. That was version two. After I released that people started wanting the ability to respond to email as well. That was version three. That process went on for a couple of years inside of Google before we released to the world.
>
> Startups don't have hundreds of internal users, so it's important to release to the world much sooner.[15]

When you develop this way, releasing early and often, you build authentic conversation right into the process. If you decide, before you even build, to evolve the software based on feedback and interaction, you're way ahead of the game.

Keep Attention by Reacting Positively to Negative Feedback

Every time something negative happens, you as a software maker have a choice: do you engage or ignore? Even in the worst-case scenario, such as the Dell Hell incident we talked about in the beginning of the chapter, it's probably better to engage and be authentic than to pretend it didn't happen.

---

15 http://paulbuchheit.blogspot.com/2008/02/most-import-thing-to-understand-about.html

The Dreamhost Debacle

The types of things that Dell went through are happening all the time now. Just recently, the web-hosting company Dreamhost accidentally overcharged its customers a hefty amount (seventy-five million dollars!) and then had to deal with the public aftermath. The results were not very good, with many folks upset at their attempt at humor, which was to use Homer Simpson as a foil.

Um, Whoops.
January 15, 2008 on 9:52 am | In Foobars, Insider View, Musings by Josh Jones |

Hello.. how's your morning going?

I hope it's been a little better than mine.

We had a *teensy eensy weensy* little billing error last night... my first clue *something* was up when I saw this morning's **daily** billing report (so far): **$7,500,000.**

It turns out due to my excessively fat fingers, **nearly every one** of our customers has been seriously over-billed in the last 12 hours.

I bet when you read this part of the last newsletter:

   4. New Office!

   Another important thing I've been doing instead of writing newsletters is looking out the window of our NEW OFFICE:

   http://blog.dreamhost.com/2007/12/21/were-so-high-right-now-you-dont-even-know

   If your next web hosting bill from us is mysteriously tripled, now you know why.

.. you thought it was a **joke!**

Ha, the **joke is on you!** I guess. Um, okay, no, not really, I'm sorry.

How on earth could something like this happen?

Figure 3.5 After Dreamhost overcharged its customers $75 million and posted about it with a humorous image of Homer Simpson with a fat finger, few people found Dreamhost's attempt at humor funny.

But even though Dreamhost took a hard beating over their blunder and their blog post, all was not lost. Even when things blow up, it's important to remember that it's only one negative incident in what is hopefully a long line of positive ones.

Secret #1: It's Over Quick

Consider this comment left by an unhappy Dreamhost customer:

> Here are some awesome things I'm thankful for:
>
> Thanks for the cheap prices.
>
> Thanks for the awful service.
>
> Thanks for the awful blog posts.
>
> Thanks for the awful customer service.
>
> Thanks for having inappropriate images on your homepage.
>
> Thanks for causing mass headache for thousands of your customers.
>
> Thanks for being awful enough for me to realize to switch to a real webhost.
>
> Thanks for making such an obvious mistake so that everyone is alerted to your poor service.[16]

The question is: how long does this person stick around? Not long. They obviously have a mean streak, and while they were a valued customer, they're not being entirely fair about the issue. If people are really upset, they're gone quickly. Better to take it on the chin and quickly resolve to make the situation better.

Secret #2: People are Cool with Hiccups

Surprisingly, most people are reasonable and are cool with hiccups in your service, as long as you acknowledge them and are honest in dealing with them. That's where authenticity comes to your aid. It's actually OK to screw up as long as you're not trying to deceive people about what happened. The Homer Simpson reference was straddling that line.

This guy wasn't even a Dreamhost customer, but now he puts them on the top of the list just for responding like they did!

> I've been working on a site for some time, and looking at different hosts. Well this post just put you at the top of the list. No excuses, no blameshifting, and immediately trying to fix what went wrong. Yeah it's a hassle for people, but from the sound of it you guys are working hard to put everything right again. sometimes the measure of a company isn't in how many mistakes you find, but how they handle them when they are found. Kudos

---

16 http://blog.dreamhost.com/2008/01/15/um-whoops/

Secret #3: It's the Average that Matters

Another secret is that, like most human relationships, it's the average over time that matters. If you have built strong relationships with your customers in the past, you probably have them on your side. So even if trolls come through and try to tear your reputation to shreds over a single incident, other people will come to your defense. Consider this Dreamhost customer's response to the comments:

> As a dreamhost customer, I think they have been/are doing a good job. Circumstances like this have to be foreseen, and like mentioned before, you have to have a fallback plan ALWAYS. You shouldn't have everything hinging on one solution, thats bad business practice. Besides, with Dreamhost youre probably saving/have saved much more than you lost through this, had you going with another provider. A mistake is a mistake, time to correct it and move on. Any other host would charge you 10x to begin with, before the error, and wouldnt be as willing to be frank about it, detailing exactly what happened and how. I say keep up the good work Dreamhost, and im glad to be a customer+will continue to be.[17]

How To Say You're Sorry

When you do need to say you're sorry, it's helpful to have a plan. The site perfectapology.com can help with this.

Here is their template for doing so.

1. a detailed account of the situation
2. acknowledgement of the hurt or damage done
3. taking responsibility for the situation
4. recognition of your role in the event
5. a statement of regret
6. asking for forgiveness
7. a promise that it won't happen again
8. a form of restitution whenever possible

---

17 http://blog.dreamhost.com/2008/01/15/um-whoops/

The JetBlue Apology

Perfectapology.com's perfect apology hall of fame includes the following apology[18] from JetBlue CEO David Neeleman, who bit the bullet after a winter storm caused massive confusion and cancellations for JetBlue customers. They've annotated the apology to show just what technique JetBlue used to make such an effective apology.

Dear JetBlue Customers —————————————————— *Salutation*

We are sorry and embarrassed. But most of all, we are deeply sorry.

This short statement at the top of the page expresses humility and remorse. It also sets the tone in this sample apology letter.

Last week was the worst operational week in JetBlue's seven year history. Following the severe winter ice storm in the Northeast, we subjected our customers to unacceptable delays, flight cancellations, lost baggage, and other major inconveniences. The storm disrupted the movement of aircraft, and, more importantly, disrupted the movement of JetBlue's pilot and inflight crewmembers who were depending on those planes to get them to the airports where they were scheduled to serve you. With the busy President's Day weekend upon us, rebooking opportunities were scarce and hold times at 1-800-JETBLUE were unacceptably long or not even available, further hindering our recovery efforts.

This paragraph gives a specific and detailed account of the incident and takes full responsibility for the situation.

It is worth noting that although the catalyst was a winter storm that NO blame is placed on it—full responsibility is taken by the company.

Words cannot express how truly sorry we are for the anxiety, frustration and inconvenience that we caused. This is especially saddening because JetBlue was founded on the promise of bringing humanity back to air travel and making the experience of flying happier and easier for everyone who chooses to fly with us. We know we failed to deliver on this promise last week.

Here, we see that they recognize their role in the situation and acknowledge the hurt and damage done.

We are committed to you, our valued customers, and are taking immediate corrective steps to regain your confidence in us. We have begun putting a comprehensive plan in place to provide better and more timely information to you, more tools and resources for our crewmembers and improved procedures for handling operational difficulties in the future. We are confident, as a result of these actions, that JetBlue will emerge as a more reliable and even more customer responsive airline than ever before.

continues on next page

This paragraph details their commitment to change and shows customers the preventive measures being taken to ensure that this type of situation will not happen again.

JetBlue also understands the Art of Apologizing by providing a link on their website to a video message from the CEO and author of the letter. This unique approach is what makes this a perfect sample apology letter.

The company now offers the recipients of the letter a form of restitution and compensation. This cleverly crafted commitment to change (through a Customer Bill of Rights) will shed a positive light on the company from both existing and future customers and the public at large.

---

18 http://www.perfectapology.com/how-to-say-im-sorry.html

Note how this is the first and only time in the letter where they use the word "I" as opposed to "we." This underscores the personal connection that the founder and CEO of the company is trying to establish with his customers.

This statement expresses regret and lets customers know that the company is hoping to continue the relationship.

Note how the last paragraph is "You" focused. They "humbly" give the customer back all the power.

Most importantly, we have published the JetBlue Airways Customer Bill of Rights—our official commitment to you of how we will handle operational interruptions going forward—including details of compensation. I have a video message to share with you about this industry leading action.

You deserved better—a lot better—from us last week. Nothing is more important than regaining your trust and all of us here hope you will give us the opportunity to welcome you onboard again soon and provide you the positive JetBlue Experience you have come to expect from us.

Sincerely,
David Neeleman
Founder and CEO
JetBlue Airways[19]

Treat Criticism as Opportunity

It is impossible to avoid negative criticism. Better to use it to your advantage and treat it as free suggestions for improvement, even if it is a bitter pill to swallow. You can't be perfect all the time, but you *can* show people you care all the time. JetBlue came out of their situation badly bruised, but this apology certainly helped them get back on their feet.

Dell is Well

I started this chapter by exploring the infamous Dell Hell case, where Jeff Jarvis posted his frustration with the company and the resulting aftermath where Dell showed precisely what not to do in those circumstances.

Well, Dell eventually recognized their mistake and took action to remedy it. They started several new customer support initiatives founded on the idea of having authentic conversations with their customers.

The new initiatives are paying off. Take, for example, the wonderful blog post made by Lionel Menchaca, Dell's Chief Blogger, after Dell's legal counsel asked the Consumerist blog to remove a post by a former Dell employee with information about how pricing works on the Dell web site. Like their decision to stay out of the Dell Hell situation, their decision to get in the middle of this was the wrong move. Here, Lionel apologizes authentically, and even references even references Jeff Jarvis in his post:

---

19 Original JetBlue apology analysis: http://www.perfectapology.com/sample-apology-letter.html

Now's not the time to mince words, so let me just say it... we blew it.

I'm referring to a recent blog post from an ex-Dell kiosk employee that received more attention after the Consumerist blogged about it, and even more still after we asked them to remove it.

In this case, I agree with what Jeff Jarvis had to say: instead of trying to control information that was made public, we should have simply corrected anything that was inaccurate. We didn't do that, and now we're paying for it.

I believe in the customer voice—that's why I signed up for this job in the first place. There's simply no cheating the system. When we're on the right track, folks tend to say some good things about us (or at least give us a second chance). When we mess up, they let us know quickly and vocally.[20]

Caveat Venditor

Not long after the Dell Hell situation started, Jeff Jarvis began to realize that his situation was a sign of things to come. He realized that he was in the middle of a profound change brought about by the web. People were able to band together and talk to each other, whether or not the company was listening. And in their confederacy, they were making actual changes in the marketplace. After hundreds of comments and news stories about his situation and its aftermath, he writes:

The age of caveat emptor is over.

Now the time has come when it's the seller who must beware. Caveat venditor.

A company can no longer get away with consistently offering shoddy products or service or ignoring customers' concerns and needs.

For now the customers can talk back where they can be heard. Those customers can gang up and share what they know and give their complaints volume. Of course, they can use their reviews and complaints to have a big impact on a company's reputation and business.

Public relations has to take on a new meaning. It can no longer be about the press and publicity, which just separate companies from the public they are supposed to serve.

Public relations must be about a new relationship with the public, with the public in charge.[21]

---

20 http://direct2dell.com/one2one/archive/2007/06/16/18397.aspx

21 http://www.buzzmachine.com/2005/07/01/dell-hell-seller-beware/

Conclusion

By making a solid commitment to authentic conversations and focusing on a specific community, you can connect as early as possible with the people who use your software. This is the most powerful way to spread the word about your service or product, to get people over the awareness hurdle, and ultimately make people happy to use your software.

By reacting positively to negative situations, you can treat even the most public of problems as an opportunity for improvement. With people becoming publishers in their own right like Jeff Jarvis, it's crucial to engage rather than avoid. To the people who use your software, customer service is vital and as much a part of the overall experience as any other part of the design. And it's a powerful tool to keep their attention.

The results of this unconventional marketing plan is that as people start to get interested in your software they tell others about it. They spread the word. Then you'll be lucky enough to have more problems on your hands. In the following chapters we talk about some of those nice-to-have problems.

Design for Sign-up

How to motivate people to sign up for your web app

"If you want to build a ship, don't drum up the men to gather wood, divide the work and give orders. Instead, teach them to yearn for the vast and endless sea."

—ANTOINE DE SAINT-EXUPERY

In a theoretically perfect world, the people who try your software for the first time have unlimited time on their hands: they hear about your web application, they go and find out more about it, and, discovering how valuable it is, they sign up for the service immediately. They appreciate the time and energy you've put into your work. The end result is a real, valuable connection between the maker and user.

In practice, however, we've got about eight seconds to make that connection.

Yep, we've got only the tiniest fraction of time to have the most important conversation of all: why someone should use our software. Of all the moments of interaction, this is the most important one, because it is when a person decides to start a relationship with you. It's the moment of decision, when someone answers the question: is this software worth my time?

What Are They Thinking?

Given how important this moment is, it's surprising how often what we imagine people are thinking differs from what they're actually thinking. Here's a typical disconnect:

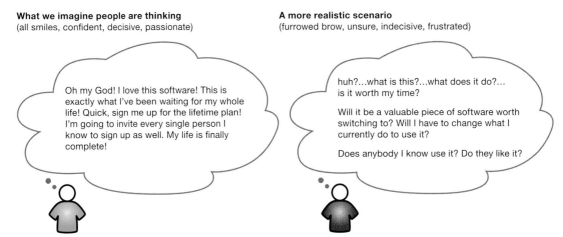

What we imagine people are thinking
(all smiles, confident, decisive, passionate)

Oh my God! I love this software! This is exactly what I've been waiting for my whole life! Quick, sign me up for the lifetime plan! I'm going to invite every single person I know to sign up as well. My life is finally complete!

A more realistic scenario
(furrowed brow, unsure, indecisive, frustrated)

huh?...what is this?...what does it do?... is it worth my time?

Will it be a valuable piece of software worth switching to? Will I have to change what I currently do to use it?

Does anybody I know use it? Do they like it?

Figure 4.1 The difference between what we hope people are thinking and what they are actually thinking is all too often quite large.

Ok, this is a *slight* exaggeration (but only slight). Our imagination is so powerful that we imbue our audience with the characteristics we want them to have: confidence, decisiveness, and passion. We want them to be really excited by our software. But, realistically, they're probably not. Most likely, even people who are interested in our software still have to be convinced before taking the plunge.

The Sign-up Hurdle

Once you have people interested, the next major challenge is to convince those interested people to actually sign up to use your software for the first time.

Interested　　　　**First-time use**

Figure 4.2 The hurdle of sign-up separates those interested in your software from those using it. This transition is marked by lots of questions and a need to clearly explain the benefits of use.

The importance of this step cannot be understated. It is crucial for several reasons:

▶ **The first, and lasting, impression**. The first impression someone has of your software is your best chance to start a person down the road of becoming a loyal user. If you lose someone in this initial transaction, they're very unlikely to return, having convinced themselves that your application isn't worth using.

▶ **All questions, few answers**. At this stage people have the most questions of all, and in answering those questions you can use the the opportunity to tell the story of your software.

▶ **Potential to kinetic energy**. At this stage people are getting ready to take their first actual steps in using your software. It's a big deal to change from the potential energy of being interested in software to the kinetic energy of actually using it.

▶ **Critical choice**. If you make a living through your web application (and many of us do), the choice people are making of whether or not to use your software is anything but trivial. They're choosing to either start a relationship with you or have it with someone else. This will undoubtedly affect your future in a big way. Therefore, it is serious business.

Different Strokes for Different Folks

Each person who visits your web application has their own agenda: they're trying to do something specific. While we don't always know what that something is, we can identify recurring roles that seem to crop up again and again. Here are some roles to watch out for:

▶ **Ready to Go.** This is the role most people design for. This is the role we hope for. These people are ready to start using your application. The key to designing for them is to get out of their way. They're already convinced your software is worth trying, so make it as easy as possible to sign up by eliminating usability problems and unnecessary friction in the interface.

▶ **Interested but Unsure**. These people are interested in your software but are unsure if it is for them. There are a lot of these people. They need to be reassured they're making the right decision in trying your software. They have specific questions about what your software can do. The key to designing for them is to provide multiple levels of detail (see section below) so that they can find appropriate answers to their questions.

▸ **Fact-finders**. These folks are doing reconnaissance and don't plan on using your software just yet. They want enough detail so they can report back to others (perhaps their colleagues, or perhaps their readership). Design for them by providing a solid summary and how-it-works information.

▸ **Skeptical**. These folks basically want to prove to themselves that your software isn't what they want. They want to find out that the software they're currently using is a better solution, so they don't have to go through the pain of switching. These folks present an interesting opportunity. Design for them by providing lots of evidence that other people are happy using your software.

Creating a Sign-up Framework

A sign-up framework is the set of information and resources we provide to people who are going to be signing up for our application. It may contain one or more of the following:

▸ An elevator pitch, a tagline, or some other pithy explanation of service

▸ Graphics or illustrations that show how your software works

▸ Carefully crafted copywriting that describes your software

▸ In-depth feature tour or feature pages

▸ Video or screencast showing actual use

▸ Get people started using the software as early as possible

▸ Evidence of other people using your software successfully

What a Good Sign-up Framework Does

The job of a sign-up framework is to help people make the jump from being interested in your software to being a first-time user.

A good sign-up framework maintains and hopefully increases any momentum a person brings with them to your application.

To maintain that momentum, a sign-up framework must do the following:

▸ Clearly communicate the capabilities of the software

▸ Allow a person to decide if the software is right for them

▸ Answer any outstanding questions people have about the software

▸ Confirm or refute any preconceptions people have about the application

▸ Get people actually using the application to get stuff done

▸ Let people connect with any other people who they might collaborate or work with

▸ Give people an idea of the type of relationship they'll have with you

The techniques below explain these issues in depth.

Keep it Simple: the Journalism Technique

Sometimes the most obvious techniques are the most effective. I've found that when designing a sign-up framework, it is useful to pretend you're a journalist. As every good journalist knows, when writing a news article you have to answer the questions Who?, What?, Where?, When?, Why?, and How? You have to pretend that your readers have never heard about the subject you're writing on.

Like journalists, web designers have a core task when designing for sign-up: they have to answer the basic inquiry questions.

The basic questions of inquiry are the most basic questions that someone has about… well, almost anything:

▸ **Who** is it for? Who is going to use it? (increasingly the answer is not "just me")

▸ **What** is it? What does it do? What are its capabilities?

▸ **Where?** Where can I use it? Is there a mobile version for using on the road?

▸ **When** can I use it? Is it browser-based, so I can access it at any time?

▸ **Why** is it important to me? Why will my life be better as a result of using this?

▸ **How** does it work? How can I take advantage of this? How do I get started?

We'll go over each one of these in turn.

Describe WHAT It Is

Steve Krug, in his wonderful book *Don't Make Me Think*,[1] laments that too often web designs don't convey the big picture: what the site is about. Steve's right: there just isn't enough description about what applications are and what they do.

Sometimes, as is the case with online invoicing application Blinksale, the answer is wonderfully obvious: "the easiest way to send invoices online." The beauty of this simple statement is that now the reader can make a decision based on whether or not sending invoices online is important to them. If it is, they can keep reading or sign up immediately. If it isn't, they've wasted at most five seconds.

Figure 4.3 Blinksale's tagline says all you need to know. It clearly answers the question "what is this?"

In addition to the simple statement of what it does, Blinksale then gets into more detail: you can send elegantly formatted invoices to anyone with an email address, use an invoice template, or import your client records. Done. You know most of what there is to know about what this application does. That is the point of a simple description like this: to drive people into learning more about it.

Now, invoicing isn't a very complicated process and Blinksale keeps it remarkably easy. So why does their competitor, billmyclients.com, make it seem so complicated?

---

1   Steve Krug, *Don't Make Me Think*, 2nd Edition. New Riders, 2006.

Figure 4.4 On Bill My Clients.com, it is possible to glean what the application is about, but it's light years away from the clarity of Blinksale.

A complicated interface suggests a complicated service.

Most of the people who see this screen are immediately drawn to the input fields asking them to log in. "Uh-oh," they think. "I don't have a login."

The funny thing is that billmyclients.com provides the same service that Blinksale does. They just aren't communicating it as clearly. You have to actually read the fine print to know what's going on. (It is there, believe me.) It says, in the small black text in the middle of the screen, that first-time users can set up an account and send an invoice for free. That's super-important information, but it's hidden in the design.

To their credit, the billmyclients site has a pretty obvious tagline: "invoicing made easy." But it's completely obscured by the design. It's not what you see first on the page, like you do on Blinksale.

So the first step is to describe what it is. The second step, just as crucial, is to put that information front and center in your design. Make it obvious like Blinksale does. Don't hide it, like Bill My Clients does.

And that's just sending invoices by email. Any more complicated web sites (i.e. most of them) are going to have an even harder time communicating what they are. Try to do this in the most straightforward, basic way possible.

Show HOW it Works

When Apple released their iPhone in the summer of 2007, they touted its touchscreen as a revolutionary new input device. They said it would change the way people interacted with computers forever.

Not everyone was convinced, however. Many people worried that the smooth-surfaced touchscreen couldn't replace the tactile feel of an actual keyboard. Understandably, people wondered if it might be difficult to type.

The speculation mounted. Would it be easy to type if there weren't physical buttons? Would you be able to type without looking? What happens when you can't feel the pressure underneath your finger? How do you correct errors?

But Apple had an answer for all this speculation: a set of videos that showed people using the iPhone. It showed people pressing buttons, dialing phone numbers, sending SMS messages. Apple called this a "Guided Tour."[2]

Figure 4.5 The video "Guided Tour" of the iPhone was remarkably successful in showing how the buttonless touchscreen could be used successfully.

As prospective buyers watched the video, all doubt of whether or not the keyboard was usable dissolved instantly. Here was video proof that you can easily type without keys—there were people doing it!

---

2   See http://www.apple.com/iphone/gettingstarted/guidedtour_large.html for the Guided Tour video.

When how-it-works features work well, like the Apple video, they do several things:

▶ Make it absolutely clear what the steps are to make it work

▶ Allay fears about the design being difficult or confusing

▶ Serve as a guide to people who want to follow step by step

▶ Illustrate how easy it can be to use your stuff

▶ Become something that your audience can pass around and share

▶ Prove that people have had success

▶ Nudge those folks who are on the fence

Netflix's Four-Pane Masterwork

A good "How It Works" graphic is short and sweet, explaining the major points of your application and nothing more. Just the facts, ma'am.

On the homepage of Netflix they have done a great job of this.

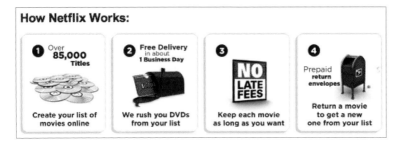

Figure 4.6 The "How Netflix Works" graphic is an excellent example of how graphics can convey a lot of important information in a small, fast package.

This graphic does several things very well:

▶ Explains what Netflix is all about in a super-fast way

▶ Embeds text within the graphic for additional clarity

▶ Assigns ownership to the viewer—"your list of movies"

▶ Shows the progression of service—what steps happen in what order

▶ Gives a clear indication of how long each step takes

▶ Explains who does what (You: create list and return movies, We: send you movies)

▶ Explains in user's language why service is different/better (no late fees)

Now, I've worked on projects where a graphic like the Netflix graphic was voted down. Here is how the discussion went:

Designer: *I think a graphic showing how the service works would help to make it really clear for people who aren't quite sure about signing up yet.*

Manager: *Well, we're an easy service to begin with, and most people know about us. Let's not muck up the homepage with information that people already know. Let's promote our latest movies instead.*

This manager obviously deals in generalities, believing that "most" people already know about their service. But the designer knows that there are people who won't be gung-ho about signing up for the service, and wants to help that specific group of people. Designing for sign-up is about planning for these contingencies, asking "what questions do people have?" and "have we provided answers for them?"

So the answer to the manager would be: "How do you think Netflix got to the point where everyone knew how easy the service was? With graphics like this, of course!"

Nobody, not even a genius, minds something being communicated absolutely clearly.

TripIt and a Second Level of Detail

Like Netflix, TripIt has an excellent graphic on their homepage that quickly conveys how the service works.

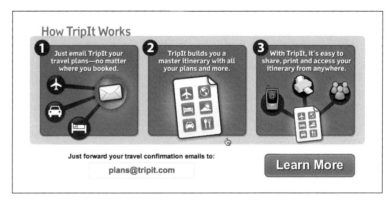

Figure 4.7 Although the "How It Works" graphic on TripIt.com provides a clear overview of the service, they go one step further and provide a second level of detail reached by clicking "Learn More."

In three panes the designers at TripIt have explained the gist of the service. Many people who were double-checking that this was the service they thought it was or were on the fence will gladly sign up after confirming how easy it is. They can simply follow the instructions to "forward your travel confirmation emails to plans@tripit.com."

But TripIt doesn't stop there. They go on to provide a second level of detail for those folks still needing to know more. This illustrates an important principle.

Good how-it-works features provide multiple levels of detail, at increasing depth of description, allowing people to dig deeper as needed.

To get to this second level of detail, they provide two options. One option is labeled "Learn More." It's a huge orange button that follows the three-pane "How It Works" section. For folks wanting to learn more about how it works, that's the clear call to action.

The second option is the more interesting one. The link is entirely different *even though it goes to the same place as the other option.* It communicates a completely different call to action.

Figure 4.8 TripIt offers multiple paths to its second level of detail, giving people options to learn about what interests them most.

Since it is not as prominent as the other call to action, this second option might not get huge numbers of people clicking on it. But for those folks who didn't follow the first path, this option offers a slightly different message.

When you do select one of these options, you're taken to what's called the "Learn more about TripIt" page. This is the second level of detail, providing deeper information about the topics already presented on the homepage.

Providing this second level of detail has several effects:

▸ Keeps the user's momentum while reinforcing the main message

▸ Answers any questions that may be left after viewing the graphic

▸ Provides more details for people still unconvinced of the service's value or wanting to know more

▶ Gives you permission to really explain in-depth some important details (i.e. you have their attention)

▶ Provides an opportunity to start naming specific features of the service. You can link to an even deeper level of detail, such as a feature tour or examples of the service in use.

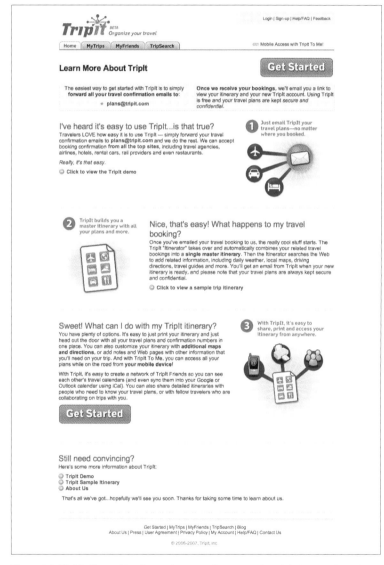

Figure 4.9 TripIt's "Learn More" page is an excellent extension of their original graphic, providing a second level of detail and explanation.

Notice that TripIt used the same graphic on their "Learn More" screen as they did on their homepage. They simply cut it up into three pieces and explained each piece. This clearly demonstrates that second level of detail.

Show the End Result

Showing how your application works is even more effective when you can show the end result. The end result of using the TripIt application, for example, is a one-page travel itinerary. This helps to make all the how-it-works information concrete. People can now see exactly how their travel information is aggregated and displayed.

Figure 4.10 TripIt's example itinerary is a great example of showing the end result. The designers even annotated the itinerary to highlight key features.

Explain WHY with Benefits as Well as Features

For years, copywriters have made the important distinction between features and benefits. Unfortunately, copywriters are often left out of the writing stages of web site development, so developers end up trying to pitch their apps on their features, not their more powerful benefits.

Features are capabilities of the system, and although they are very important, they don't explain *why* someone might use them.

Let's imagine we were building a social bookmarking tool. The *features* might be those in the left column of the following table, while the benefits are those things in the right column: the *actual value* you get from the feature.

Features	Benefits
Unlimited server space	Access from any browser, anytime
Add tags your bookmarks	Organize your bookmarks in any way you want
Add friends and see their bookmarks	Collaborate and share bookmarks with friends
Sort by tag or date	Easily refind important bookmarks later
See related bookmarks	Find relevant related content

Wufoo, an online form creation tool, has an excellent way of explaining the benefits of the application. It's a simple screen called "Top 10 Reasons to Use Wufoo."

In general, it is better to explain the benefits more than the features. However, there is one group of people who often responds better to features: techies. Techies intuitively grasp the linkage between features and benefits, and are often interested in the features because they know all about how they affect the benefits. Still, it never hurts to make those connections clear.

WuFOO

Top 10 Reasons to Use Wufoo

1. Wufoo is easy.

If you've ever used a desktop form building application, then you're familiar with complexity. If you've ever hired a programmer to make a form for you, then you're familiar with delays and communication barriers. Enter Wufoo. Wufoo enables anyone from students to secretaries to office managers the ability to publish an online form within minutes. Your forms, on your terms. Programming experience not needed.

2. Wufoo is fast.

Why wait days and weeks for someone else to build a database and all the scripts needed to just collect simple information from your form? With Wufoo, you can build, design, and collect with professionalism and personality in only a few short minutes.

3. Wufoo is fun.

Just because you're working with forms and data, doesn't mean you have to do it without personality and style. Gathering information from your users is exciting, why shouldn't your tools be exciting too?

4. Wufoo is secure.

We've done everything possible to ensure the safe keeping of your data and the data you collect. Our servers are located at 365 Main and backed up onsite and offsite—every 12 hours in Toronto and every 24 hours in Virginia. We also offer plans with 128 bit SSL encryption on form submission. We have the expertise of BitPusher, a company whose founders have experience with Napster and Netcom (among others), to ensure that everything is safe and stable on the hardware end.

Figure 4.11 Wufoo's "Top 10 Reasons to Use Wufoo" is a list of the benefits of the service. Notice that technical details of features are also there, but the benefits are highlighted.

Give Examples of WHO is Using It

Restaurant A   **Restaurant B**

Hmm...Restaurant B seems like the safer choice

Figure 4.12 Social proof is the tendency to base our decisions on the activities of others. A crowded restaurant tends to stay that way because people assume that it is crowded for a good reason.

Many times we make decisions based on social cues that we might not be fully aware of. Do you ever walk by a restaurant, see a long line at the door, and think "we should probably try that out sometime"? Or, do you ever walk by a restaurant, see that it's *empty*, and think "that's probably not worth going to"? Most people do. Restaurants know this too—they'll seat early customers close to windows and encourage long lines so that passers-by see them and assume the place is worth going to.

People respond to the activity of others. So give a sense that *real* people are using your social web application. Show that others are there. Make it seem like a crowded restaurant. This leverages the powerful notion of "social proof."

Social Proof

Many of the examples in this chapter center around the idea of *social proof.* When faced with a situation in which our choice of behavior isn't clear—as in "Should we use this web app?"—we exhibit a tendency to rely on social proof. In these cases, we often look for clues in others' behavior to help us decide what our own should be.

Robert Cialdini, whose book *Influence: the Psychology of Persuasion* has been one of the most-cited psychology books of all time, has lots to teach us about how to do this. He notes that social proof is powerful even despite our awareness of it.

For example, laugh tracks on television are reviled my most people. Yet, study after study has shown that people laugh more and laugh harder when they watch shows with laugh tracks. It seems as if we can't help but be swept up with everyone else, even when we try not to be. Social proof is *that* powerful.

So to make a person's decision easier, show them how others have made the same decision and succeeded. Give *evidence* that others are using it.

Some ways to do this are described below.

Let People Find Friends

While social proof works even when we're observing perfect strangers, it is most influential when the people doing the activity in question are people we know. When someone knows that their friend is already using an application, they'll likely be undeterred in signing up. In those cases your job is easy—just get out of their way.

In some cases, people will want to know if their friends are already a part of the service before they sign up. Provide an easy and powerful search for those who want to find their friends.

Facebook is really good at this. They give two options to find friends: looking them up with your existing web-based email accounts, or doing a name search.

Figure 4.13 Facebook lets people find friends easily, allowing people to search even if they aren't signed up for the service.

Facebook is clever. In addition to search functionality, they offer a "Find Your Friends" feature that takes an email address from a web-based email account (like Gmail, Yahoo! Mail, or Hotmail), goes out and looks at your contacts on that email platform, and then gives you results.

Figure 4.14 Facebook's "Find Your Friends" function. A clever way to let people know if their friends are already on the service.

Their search feature works really well. If one of my friends were considering signing up for the service but wanted to know if I was already there, they might type in "joshua porter," and Facebook, recognizing both variants of the name, returns results for both "joshua porter" and "josh porter."

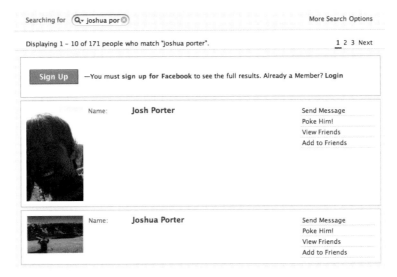

Figure 4.15 Facebook's search works well, returning variants of "joshua" in the result. They don't show you all results, however, prompting you to sign up for that.

In addition, Facebook only shows you partial search results for these queries. For example, they only show 30 of the 171 results available. This gives a tantalizing preview to the number of people you can find on the service, and increases your momentum to sign up. So even if your friend isn't on the service, you won't know until you sign up. Very clever design.

Provide Testimonials: "I love your stuff"

What someone else says about you is more important than what you say about yourself. Testimonials have long been known in advertising as gold. Even so, testimonials are still under-utilized by almost all sites.

A great example of the prodigious use of testimonials is the Basecamp site. Basecamp is project management software for groups. The designers of the site separate the testimonials onto their own page called "Buzz." It is hard to view this page and not be drawn in by the sheer number of positive comments. You can't help but think "if so many people are so positive about this software, it's got to be good."

This page, which contains 90! testimonials, also raises the question "how many testimonials is too many?" And, judging by the effectiveness of the page, maybe even ninety isn't too many.

Notice the designers place the most compelling testimonials at the top. The first testimonial is actually from a competitor! The second one is a testimonial with ties to a recognized authority (Microsoft—also a possible competitor), which carries more weight than a person from a company you've never heard about.

Figure 4.16 The Basecamp Buzz page seems like overkill as it contains 90! testimonials. But once you start reading them, you can't help but think "this is great software."

> ### Basecamp is the best out there
>
> "Thanks for the great software. It's the best out there...and I helped start a company called intranets.com, if that counts for anything."
>
> -Mark Goodstein, co-founder of Intranets.com (a Basecamp competitor)
>
> ### Basecamp is the first product I have seen that is truly project management for everyone
>
> "I worked in the project management software industry for nearly fifteen years and Basecamp is the first product I have seen that is truly project management for everyone. Nice to see someone finally figured it out."
>
> -Jim Dunnigan, **Former Product Manager Microsoft Project**

Figure 4.17 The designers of Basecamp strategically chose compelling testimonials to place at the top of the page.

Here are some other insights that the Basecamp Buzz page gives us to use when displaying testimonials:

▸ Place the most seductive at the top

▸ Place recognized authorities in more prominent places

▸ Leverage strong brands

▸ Give interesting details about the person

▸ Pull testimonials from reviews and then link to the reviews

▸ Emphasize the most compelling part of the testimonial

So, elicit testimonials. Ask people for them. More often than not, your users will be happy to share their opinion of your software. Write them down and put them on your web site. It's such a simple thing to do that it simply gets overlooked.

In addition, this also shines some attention on the people who gave you the testimonial, showing them that you value their opinion. They might even reference your acknowledgement with others, driving *even more* people to your highly effective page. So imagine that two in ten people you acknowledge are going to link to you if you publish their testimonial. Wouldn't it be better to have a hundred testimonials and get twenty incoming links than having five testimonials and one incoming link?

Get As Specific As You Can

Question: *Who is the audience you're targeting?*
Wrong Answer: *Well, anyone, really. Our application has a broad set of uses.*
Right Answer: *People who do this very specific activity…*

This is a discussion I had with an entrepreneur who was starting a new software company. He was targeting his software at what he called "the general public." And on the surface of things, this makes sense. He didn't want to limit his software by saying that it was for a particular audience, as that would make it harder to swim with the current if that strategy didn't work out. (Investors like flexibility, too.) For whatever reason, his software ended up being for all audiences.

In practice, however, software built for the masses *rarely* works. Even in cases where software has gone to the masses, it started off in a niche and then grew outward, as people realized that it doesn't have to be used in any one way.

Targeting a broad audience is precisely the wrong approach. The more specific you can get about how to use your application, the more your software will resonate with your potential audience.

Del.icio.us, the social bookmarking tool, is about as broad a tool as you can get. Anybody who wants to bookmark web pages can use it. That is to say that their potential audience is everyone on the web.

But Del.icio.us doesn't fall into the trap of designing for everyone. They do a very good job providing specific use cases.

And, if your software is flexible and can be used by many different types of audiences, choose a few profitable/big ones and be specific about each. The more specific you can get, the better.

What can I use del.icio.us for?

del.icio.us is an open-ended system, so you decide how you want to use it. Here are examples of things you can do with saving bookmarks on del.icio.us:

- **Research** - Writing an article? Researching an industry? Slaving away on your dissertation? Use del.icio.us to keep track of all the source materials and commentary that you find online.

- **Wishlist** - Go to any commerce site, find what you like, save it to del.icio.us and tag it as wishlist. Then you can tell people to check out your wishlist bookmarks by giving them a link to http://del.icio.us/*username*/wishlist .

- **Podcast** - Want to hear some great podcasts? Visit the mp3+podcast tag combination and start listening. Are you a podcaster? Start posting your mp3 files to del.icio.us and we will create an RSS feed for you.

- **Vacation** - Planning a trip? Save links to hotels, activities, and transportation and use tags like "travel", "vacation", and "to-visit". Collaborate with friends and family by using the "for:username" tag.

- **Linklog** - Save bookmarks to interesting websites and add a bit of commentary to create a lightweight linklog. Then, use linkrolls or the daily blog posting feature to include your del.icio.us bookmarks on your blog or website.

- **Cookbook** - Whenever you find a great recipe on a website, save it to del.icio.us. Tag it with the recipe's ingredients or style of cooking, and then when you're wondering what to make for dinner, you can use your saved bookmarks to help you remember the perfect recipe.

- **Collaboration** - Friends, coworkers, and other groups can use a shared account, special tag, or their del.icio.us networks to collect and organize bookmarks that are relevant -- and useful -- to the entire group.

Figure 4.18 Del.icio.us is a flexible tool that can be used by anybody. Still, the designers describe very specific use-cases when communicating its value. This is helpful for people trying to learn about it for the first time.

Success Stories/Case Studies

Even more powerful than suggesting what people can use your software for is actually showing how someone has successfully used it. Any activity seems easier if someone else has done it first.

Apple does a good job with case studies with the "profiles" feature on their professional site. They profile a successful professional and explain how that person uses Apple computers in their work. This is not a hard sell: Apple simply explains what the person uses Macs for.

Lincoln Schatz
Random Access Portraits

11/02/07 Lincoln Schatz's generative videos take the pose out of portraiture... **Read More**

Qian Qian
Drawing from the East

10/26/07 Wielding a Mac and a mouse, Chinese-born, New York–based designer Qian Qian produces illustrations and graphic designs that reach... **Read More**

Les Paul
Invented Here

10/19/07 In a forthcoming DVD set, legendary guitarist and recording pioneer Les Paul takes us behind the scenes of his 50s TV/radio hit "the... **Read More**

Show More Profiles

Figure 4.19 On Apple's professional site, they offer "profiles" (case studies) to show how people are using Macs in their work.

Successful case studies tend to:

▸ Show how real people (even famous ones) use your application successfully

▸ Sound like a genuine study of use, rather than an advertisement

▸ Talk in depth about the activity at hand, without resorting to generalities

▸ Can get really technical about how the application is used (the text of Apple's profiles goes into good depth about what the person uses their software and hardware for.)

In the past few years, though still remarkably busy, Paul found time to organize his video and audio archives, with help from research assistant Elliott Liggett. "We decided to restore the Listerine shows, which were recorded optically," says Paul. "Luckily, I'd kept all the audio masters that had been edited for these shows on magnetic tape. And so when we decided to take these first 140 shows and change them all over to the optical tracks, we had to do what I call a car wash. To clean them up and make sure that they're in sync, and that the quality was very good."

Liggett suggested that for this car wash the "natural tool would be a Mac." And when Liggett returned to school, engineer Jim Krause took over readying the archival footage for DVD. The original 5-minute Listerine shows, originally shot on film (which contains both optical audio and video tracks) had at some point been transferred to 1-inch tape. After moving the tapes into Final Cut Pro on a Mac using the AJA IO, Krause began replacing the poor quality optical audio tracks with the better quality audio from the stored magnetic tapes. He then synced the audio with the video, even adjusting video timing as necessary.

Figure 4.20 Apple's case studies focus on how their products make sense for the activity at hand, getting into some of the details that most people wouldn't know.

Case studies are the ultimate in detail. They are where you can dive into more complicated issues than most people, except those few who are interested in the very specific activity, will understand.

Give Numbers (When They're Big)

"99 Billion Served." Most McDonald's restaurants claim that unfathomable number of people served. It says "an amazing number of people have eaten here."

Software companies can do this as well. AdaptiveBlue uses the number of downloads of their software effectively. They proudly advertise that their toolbar has been downloaded over one million times. It suggests that lots of people are downloading — and they are!

Figure 4.21 A person reading this download statistic from AdaptiveBlue can't help but say "Wow, this is popular" and give it a second glance.

It's a bird, it's a plane!... it's... a window?

It might seem a silly thing to focus on numbers, but research demonstrates that people really do follow the crowd.

A classic research study on social proof is one conducted by Stanley Milgram, Leonard Bickman, and Lawrence Berkowitz in the sixties in which they had people stand on a sidewalk in New York City and look up at a sixth floor window. They recorded how many people passing by stopped and looked up as well.

If there were no such thing as social proof, nobody else would stop to look. But the results showed the real influence of this principle. When there was only a single person on the sidewalk looking up, just four percent of people passing by did the same. When the researchers put five people on the sidewalk looking up, the number more than quadrupled to eighteen percent. When they put fifteen people looking up, forty percent of people passing by couldn't help but do the same. When the number of people looking increased, passers-by were more likely to stop and look. They were compelled by the power of social proof.

Appeal to Authority

If someone with authority uses your software, it makes sense to leverage that fact by talking about how they use it. On the AdaptiveBlue site, for example, they promote their software by explaining how Seth Godin, an authority in the marketing world, uses their SmartLinks feature.

SmartLinks for Books

Seth Godin, marketing guru and best selling author, uses SmartLinks to promote his books.

Are you a reader or an author?
Check out SmartLinks for books »

Figure 4.22 If a well-known authority uses your software, tell people! This element from AdaptiveBlue doesn't oversell Seth Godin's involvement, it simply lets people know that he uses to the software to promote his books.

The Power of Authority

Authority, the ability to give order and enforce obedience, is an extremely powerful social influencer. The most famous social psychology experiment involving authority is a study by Stanley Milgram done in the early 1960s, in which he, as the authority figure, ordered people to inflict electric shocks on others, even as the others cried out in pain. A remarkable number of people simply followed the orders. (The experiment was set up to make it appear as if the subjects were really being shocked; they weren't.) Nevertheless, the results of that single study have reverberated for decades, completely reshaping how psychologists view authority. Says Milgram:

> The legal and philosophic aspects of obedience are of enormous importance, but they say very little about how most people behave in concrete situations. I set up a simple experiment at Yale University to test how much pain an ordinary citizen would inflict on another person simply because he was ordered to by an experimental scientist. Stark authority was pitted against the subjects' [participants'] strongest moral imperatives against hurting others, and, with the subjects' [participants'] ears ringing with the screams of the victims, authority won more often than not. The extreme willingness of adults to go to almost any lengths on the command of an authority constitutes the chief finding of the study and the fact most urgently demanding explanation.

> Ordinary people, simply doing their jobs, and without any particular hostility on their part, can become agents in a terrible destructive process.

> Moreover, even when the destructive effects of their work become patently clear, and they are asked to carry out actions incompatible with fundamental standards of morality, relatively few people have the resources needed to resist authority.[3]

---

3   See http://en.wikipedia.org/wiki/Milgram_experiment for the fascinating details of the Milgram experiment.

Authority works because it makes people pay attention. The mere fact that Seth Godin uses this software is impressive. But notice, too, that this element doesn't overplay Godin's involvement. It simply states that he uses the software. More importantly, it describes what he uses it for: to promote his books. That's enough information to grab those folks who might use it for the same purpose. You can bet that people who are interested in promoting their books are very interested in how Seth Godin uses this product.

Hypotheticals Are OK

If you're early on in launching your software, you may not yet have many people using it. In this case it might make sense to give people hypothetical ways to use it.

A good example is Backpack (created by 37signals, who also created Basecamp). In promoting Backpack, the design team came up with a bunch of hypothetical example uses. This is a great way to get people thinking about how best to use the software if they aren't sure.

Backpack works great for personal and business use
Plan and organize a wedding or special event • List items for sale • Organize and prepare for a meeting • Book reviews, product reviews, whatever reviews • Storing canned emails • Proposing and selecting fonts • Organize your employee searches • Publish and organize guitar tabs • Plan for your holiday greeting cards • Organize a craft project • Comparison shop and research a product on a Backpack page • Organizing a business trip • Keep track of your favorite wines (and wines you want to try) • Organize rebates, coupons, and special deals • Your favorites in your city • Use Reminders so you don't forget the little things • Presenting color palette options • New feature ideas, brainstorms, and screenshots • Quick access to numbers you need

---

Figure 4.23 A list of hypothetical uses for the app Backpack. This list gets people thinking about how it might be useful for them.

WHEN Can People Use It? Now!

Sometimes it seems as if all web software is free nowadays. But if you offer a pay-for application, consider offering a way for people to try it out for free. This is a great way for people to get excited about your service without first having to make a hard decision about budgeting or pricing.

Letting people try out your application also has an interesting effect. By giving people something for free, you've evoked the feeling of *reciprocation*: people are much more likely to stick with you for it. You've given them something for free, and they're more likely to give something in return (their business).

Goplan, a project management application, offers a version of their software that anybody can try for free. It is a limited version without some of the bells and whistles of the more expensive plans, but is enough to get you started and pique your interest. Sometimes people don't realize the value of something until they've actually used it.

	Unlimited $100/month	Professional $50/month	Startup $20/month	Personal $10/month	Free Free
Projects at once	Unlimited	100	30	12	2 (*)
Users per project	Unlimited	Unlimited	Unlimited	8	4
Storage space	25 GB	6 GB	1.5 GB	300 MB	15 MB
User permissions	Included	Included	Included	Included	N/A
Calendar and Chat	Included	Included	Included	Included	N/A
256-bit SSL	Included	Included	Included	Included	N/A

Figure 4.24 Goplan offers a free version of their project management application. It's a great way to get people hooked on your software.

Reciprocity

Robert Cialdini's book *Influence: The Psychology of Persuasion* (mentioned previously in this chapter) also talks about the power of reciprocity. Many of us are familiar with it even if we don't use that term to describe it. Think of the unexpected Christmas gift you received that made you feel guilty for not being able to reciprocate with a gift in kind.

Cialdini notes that reciprocity can be used for both good and bad. Being "indebted" to someone else is a horrible thing if you don't feel a mutual respect. An obvious example is seen in mob movies all the time: the mobster will do a "favor" for an unwitting person out of the blue, and all will be well until the mobster wants something in return. Then the recipient of the gift feels compelled to comply with the mobster's wishes.

Cialdini adds that it might be the most powerful way to influence others:

> One of the reasons reciprocation can be used so effectively as a device for gaining another's compliance is its power. The rule possesses awesome strength, often producing a "yes" response to a request that, except for an existing feeling of indebtedness, would have surely been refused. [4]

---

4   Robert Cialdini, *Influence: The Psychology of Persuasion*. Quill William Morrow, 1984.

WHERE Can People Use Your Application?

Until recently, the question of "where" you can use web applications wasn't that interesting. However, expanding mobile phone use is changing that, allowing people to use web applications anywhere they can use their phone.

In some cases, mobile access changes the entire value proposition of social software. Consider the case of Google Maps, a mapping platform that becomes much more useful when you're on the go.

The Maps design team has done a good job of explaining the benefits of using their application while on the move.

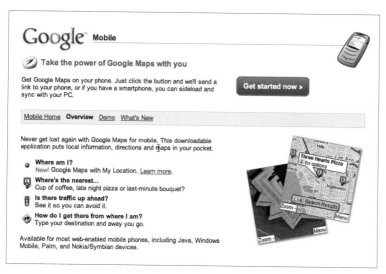

Figure 4.25 The mobile page for Google Maps is a good example of highlighting some of the interesting uses of their application while on the move.

The secret to designing for mobile use is *context*. What sorts of activities are people going to use your software for when they're on the move? If the answer is a specific set of activities like on Google Maps, it makes sense to call these out specifically.

Reduce Sign-up Friction

So now we've answered a person's basic questions about our web application. In some cases we focused on what value the application provides, while in others we focused on more social issues like who is using it. The journalism technique covers most of those bases.

If we've done our job right, people are motivated to take the next step and use the application. With luck we've now got everyone in the "Ready to Go" mindset. The key at this point is to reduce sign-up friction as much as possible.

Don't Make Creating an Account a Requirement (until You Need to)

Just forward your travel confirmation emails to:
plans@tripit.com

Figure 4.26 TripIt makes starting a snap. All you have to do is forward an existing email to the service and they create an itinerary for you.

TripIt.com has an excellent way to get started using their service with very little friction. Say you book at flight at Orbitz.com. You'll get an email from them confirming your flight details. Simply forward that email to plans@tripit.com and they create a page for your itinerary. They send you an email back with a link to your newly-created page. You've essentially started using their application without creating an account, or even visiting the site!

Another great example is Netvibes, a web-based desktop application. They invite you to start using their service immediately by configuring your own desktop.

Netvibes makes creating an account seem almost like an afterthought. They provide value way before they make you sign up. Here's the text:

> This is your personalized page, you can now modify everything: move modules, add new RSS/ATOM feeds, change the parameters for each module, etc. Your modifications are saved in real-time and you'll find your page when you get back on Netvibes.com. If you want to be able to access your page from any computer, you can sign in (at the top right) with your email and a password.

The Netvibes example highlights a larger principle of form design. I don't know if it is written in stone somewhere, but it should be:

Upon signup, ask only for information that's absolutely necessary

In the case of Netvibes, *nothing* is required to start using their application. Talk about a frictionless process. Only after you start using it do they remind you that if you want to save what you've done, you have to sign up.

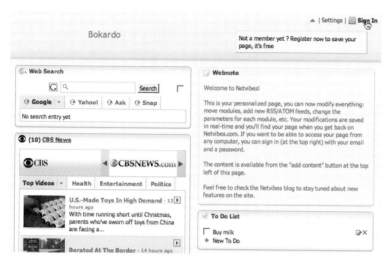

Figure 4.27 Netvibes kindly lets you play with the tool before having to create an account. In fact, they almost make creating an account seem like an afterthought... what a novel idea!

Progressive Engagement

Interface designer Luke Wroblewski calls this technique progressive engagement.[5] Progressive engagement allows people to get started using software without committing fully or filling out a sign-up form. They engage with the software slowly instead of having to scale the hurdle of a sign-up form before engaging.

Both Netvibes and Tripit practice progressive engagement. Contrast the experience of those sites with that of the *Wall Street Journal*. When reading an article snippet on wsj.com, you're asked to subscribe to the service for full access. When you press "subscribe," you're presented with a daunting form. Not only do you have to pay money (a hurdle in itself), not only does this form contain more fields than necessary, but it's only one of four pages!

Now, someone might argue that "It's the *Wall Street Journal*, the most respected newspaper in the world, so they can do what they want." Not so. What the *Wall Street Journal* has done is to increase signup friction. The only way to overcome that increased friction is to increase motivation by using the techniques mentioned above. While readers

---

5   Luke explores progressive engagement in his book: *Web Form Design: Filling in the Blanks* http://www.rosenfeldmedia.com/books/webforms/

of the *Wall Street Journal* might be highly motivated, that shouldn't be a requirement just to fill out a form!

Figure 4.28 The *Wall Street Journal* has an incredible amount of friction in their signup process. This daunting form is only one of four pages!

Conclusion

The moment a person signs up for your software is crucial: it's the moment when they decide to start a relationship with you. If it's a bad experience and they can't quite muster up the motivation to sign up, they may never return.

By using the simple and effective journalism technique to answer the basic questions of inquiry, you can go a long way to getting (or keeping) people motivated to use your software.

In the next chapter we'll talk about keeping that momentum during actual use of your software and helping people get up to speed with regular use.

Design for Ongoing Participation

How to keep people happy and participating over the long term

"Even a casual trip through cyberspace will turn up evidence of hostility, selfishness, and simple nonsense. Yet the wonder of the Internet is not that there is so much noise, but that there is any significant cooperation at all. Given that online interaction is relatively anonymous, that there is no central authority, and that it is difficult or impossible to impose monetary or physical sanctions on someone, it is striking that the Internet is not literally a war of all against all."[1]

—PETER KOLLOCK, PROFESSOR OF SOCIOLOGY, UCLA

---

1   Peter's research and writing on online motivation is fantastic, supporting many of the ideas in this chapter. You can find out more about his work at: http://www.sscnet.ucla.edu/soc/faculty/kollock/

So you've started having authentic conversations (Chapter 3), and you've optimized your screens for sign-up (Chapter 4). You're generating good will and clearly communicating the value of your service.

The hard part is over, right?

Well, no. While those initial steps are important, they only help someone get up to speed. Once they start using your web app on a regular basis, all that initial momentum goes out the window. The honeymoon phase of software is over in a hurry. The *really* high hurdle is ahead: keeping people regularly visiting your site over the long term.

Return visits

First-time use   **Regular use**

Figure 5.1 To get people using your web app regularly, you need to motivate them appropriately and design interfaces that encourage those motivations.

The difficulty of this problem explains why I hear the following about once a week:

> We launched our web application a few months ago. We had good initial interest, lots of people signed up at first. But that has dropped off and instead of growing steadily, our usage is barely rising. We're having trouble simply getting people to participate. How do we encourage that?

Contrary to popular belief, the answer is *not* more advertising or more features or more funding.

The answer is *motivation.*

If you can discover how to motivate people in the right way, then you don't need those stopgaps. If you pay attention to and take care of the people on your site, you will do just fine. The investors, advertisers, and features will come in time. Those will be symptoms of success, not causes of it! The cause of success will be a happy population of people who love your software.

There are two parts to getting ongoing participation right:

1. **Identifying the right motivations for use.** Understand why people are participating in the first place

2. **Creating interfaces that support and encourage those motivations.** Interfaces elicit participation by supporting those motivations appropriately

Let's explore the core motivations for participation and how to create interfaces to support them. First, the primary question.

Why Do People Participate?

At first it would seem like there are countless reasons to participate online. After all, we do a million things on the web, from serious business to mindless fun.

However, while the activities we do *are* very different—as we discussed in Chapter 2—the basic reasons why we do each of them *are not*. Most people participate for relatively common reasons. For example, many people write reviews on Amazon because of a feeling of reciprocity—they recognize the value they get from the site and want to give back. Others write reviews out of a sense of efficacy, as they feel the urge to tell others about their experience so as to help them make a tough decision.

The key, then, is to identify the basic motivational model—the two or three core motivations—of your users and spend most of your design energy building out your software to support them.

Here's a list of motivations that I'll spend the rest of the chapter exploring. Notice that I've left out the common reason we think motivates people: money (economic capital). As I mentioned in Chapter 1, social design is not about economic but social capital. That's what these motivations are all about.

▶ **Identity**. People use social web apps to manage their identity within their social groups

▶ **Uniqueness**. People use social web apps because they feel that their contribution is unique and valuable

▶ **Reciprocity**. People participate because they either want to give back or because they expect others to give back to them

▶ **Reputation**. People participate to build their reputation and improve their relationships with others

▶ **Sense of efficacy**. People participate in order to do good work and have a positive effect

▶ **Control**. People want control over how their information is shared and displayed

▶ **Ownership**. People participate because they feel a sense of ownership over their content online

- **Attachment to a group**. People seek to find like-minded people who share the same values and/or activities
- **Fun**. It's fun to participate and play!

The following design tactics are ways to motivate people that are all born of regular human interaction. They are not tricks. If we asked people who participate in social web sites, they might recognize these principles in action. Some might even agree and say "Yep, that's what I'm doing. I'm trying to build my reputation on this service."

Enable Identity Management

Everyone has an identity. Identity is what makes us who we are. Identity is the sum of the characteristics we recognize each other by. Eye color, height, personality, physical abilities, intelligence: these are some of the things that make up our identity. We take this identification for granted in the offline world.

Online, on the other hand, we have the freedom to represent ourselves in any way we choose. Since we're not interacting face-to-face, we have total control over what identifying information we present.

Online identity can be as simple as a username or as complex as a personalized profile page and set of social relationships. By providing people with tools to identify themselves and interact with others, we *enable identity*.

The power of identity

What happens when a site *doesn't* have it? When identity isn't enabled, you tend to get:

- **SPAM.** People sending unsolicited messages to large numbers of others
- **Gaming.** People using the system in ways it wasn't intended
- **Comment trolls**. People leaving inappropriate comments in an attempt to ruffle feathers
- **Deception**. People pretending to be somebody they are not

In general, a lack of identity leads to bad behavior. Without a clear form of identity, there is no way to hold someone accountable, and thus no way to punish (or reward) them for their behavior.

Accounts

Most social web sites require the people who use them to create an account, which consists of a username or email identifier. When this simple "handle" is exposed in the interface, say next to a comment, it goes a long way toward providing a basic level of identity.

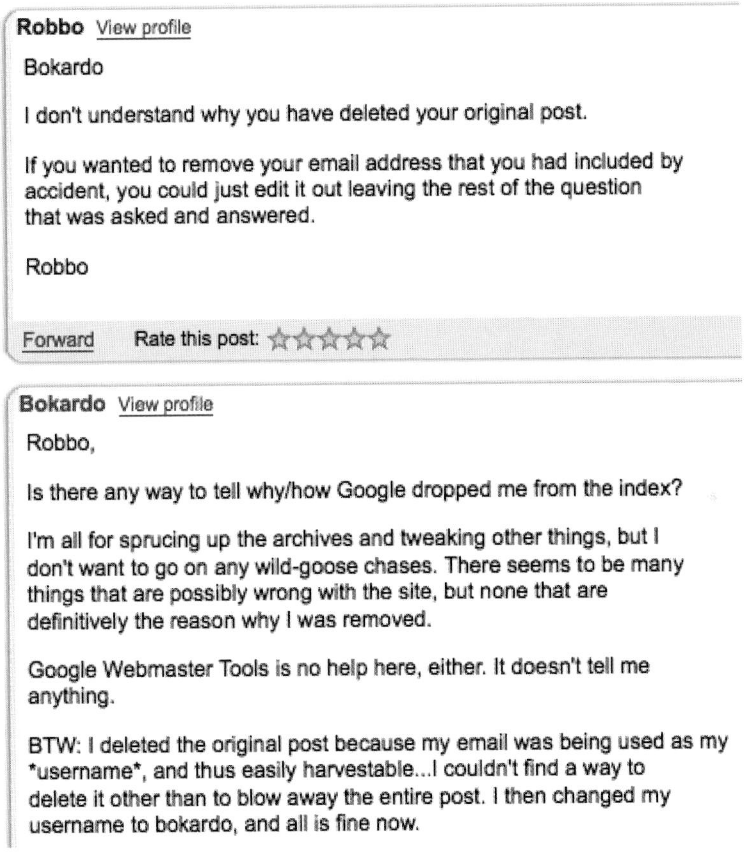

Figure 5.2 Google Groups shows a simple handle next to each post. This is enough to carry on a conversation with someone over time.

With a handle, people can identify each other enough to:

▶   Have a conversation with someone

▶   Build up a history and remember that person over time

▶   Refer to that person when speaking with others

As we mentioned in the last chapter, making accounts mandatory makes the sign-up process more difficult. It acts as a barrier to entry. An account allows the site owner to remove someone from a system when they do bad things. In some cases, however, it can't stop ne'er-do-wells. People who are really dedicated can simply create a new account.

Now, this raises the question, won't people simply pretend to be somebody else?

Actually, people don't do that very often. Clay Shirky explains one case in particular, in which a woman portrayed a sick teenager[2] and was vehemently denounced by the readership she had established:

> You see things like the Kaycee Nicole story, where a woman in Kansas pretended to be a high school student, and then because the invented high school student's friends got so emotionally involved, she then tried to kill the Kaycee Nicole persona off. "Oh, she's got cancer and she's dying and it's all very tragic." And of course, everyone wanted to fly to meet her.
>
> Now a number of people point to this and say "See, I told you about that identity thing!" But the Kaycee Nicole story is this: changing your identity is really weird. And when the community understands that you've been doing it and you're faking, that is seen as a huge and violent transgression. And they will expend an astonishing amount of energy to find you and punish you. So identity is much less slippery than [naysayers] would lead us to believe.[3]

Profile Pages

Profile pages are public or semi-public pages that identify someone (or something) within a social application. They are a collection of information about a person, group, or organization. Profile pages are initially created out of the information a person enters when they sign up for an account, but usually contain much more information that people add over time.

Profile pages often contain several of the following:

▸ A unique avatar (photo/handle) (should be large enough to identify the person)

▸ A short biography or about section

▸ Appropriate demographics (age, location, etc.)

▸ Activities or accomplishments

3   This is an excerpt from Clay Shirky's now classic (and must-read) piece "A group is its own worst enemy" http://www.shirky.com/writings/group_enemy.html

▶ A list of the latest activities involving the person

▶ Likes/dislikes

▶ Friends list

▶ Group affiliations

The Profile Has to Fit the Domain

Profiles work best when the elements they contain are aligned with the purpose of the application. Following are three examples of profiles from *very* different domains. Each is tailored for a particular purpose.

Profiles on LinkedIn, a social networking application for business professionals, contain information suited to professional interaction, like places worked, education, former and current colleagues, and professional skills. You won't see information like religious denomination, sexual preference, or someone's medical condition or other information inappropriate in a professional setting.

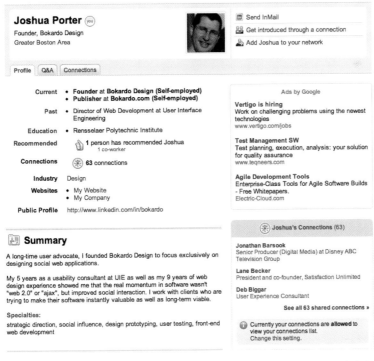

Figure 5.3 Profiles on LinkedIn are kept to business-related information. You won't find favorite movies or religious preference here.

On PatientsLikeMe, a site for people with similar medical conditions, the profiles are very different from those on LinkedIn. On a profile of somebody with multiple sclerosis, for example, you might find out important dates like when they first had symptoms or when they were diagnosed. The "about me" section focuses on their experience with the disease, while several graphing tools show how their treatment is progressing.

Unlike LinkedIn, professional information is largely irrelevant when talking about someone's medical condition, so you won't see that information mentioned in a PatientsLikeMe profile.

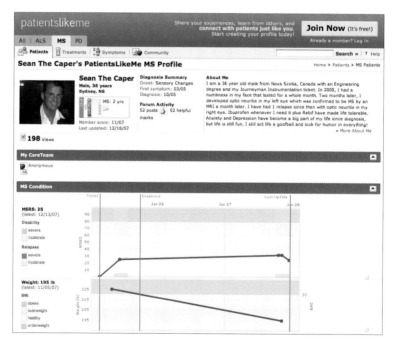

Figure 5.4 Profiles on PatientsLikeMe.com, a site for people with similar medical conditions, appropriately display relevant medical information.

Similarly, the information within profile pages on Amazon have little overlap with those of LinkedIn and PatientsLikeMe. The Amazon profile shows all your latest activity on Amazon, including items you've added to your wish list, any reviews you've written, and what your friends have done on the site.

Figure 5.5 Profiles on Amazon have everything to do with your activity on that site. There is no professional information or medical information as on LinkedIn or PatientsLikeMe, respectively.

These three examples illustrate how specialized profile pages can be. It would be easy for each of these sites to ask for more comprehensive information about each person, but that would make them end up looking like a general-purpose social network site. Competing with Facebook and MySpace is not the primary purpose of these sites. Instead, they are well-structured for their specific niche.

Show What's Happening

As social web applications became more popular over the last few years, designers started to realize that profiles suffer from being too static. If the information on them doesn't change quickly enough, they become uninteresting. And, if you're reading biographical information about an existing friend, not much of it is going to be new to you. In other words, profiles grow old fast.

Therefore, several new features that display dynamic content have emerged to address the problem.

▶ **Lifestream.** Aggregates and displays the latest activity from all sources

▶ **Comment wall.** A list of comments left by visitors for all to see

▶ **Status.** A small statement that describes your current status (e.g. "writing a chapter in my new book")

▶ **Notifications.** An announcement that something of interest has happened (invitations, birthdays, holidays)

Simply showing what's happening is a great way to garner interest. These elements cause the profile to change often, which is much more interesting than the same old content.

Watch Out for "Social Network Fade"

A word of warning about profiles. Managing profiles isn't itself a reason for an application to exist. If managing profiles is the only activity your social app is supporting, you probably won't last long. You'll end up like the people who used Friendster, of which a product manager said, "There really wasn't much to do once you set up your network and found your old friends."[4]

I call this *social network fade*. It happens when there is a rush of energy to fill out a profile upon sign-up and then a gradual fade-away after that. The fade continues until the person simply has no reason to come back. They've added all their friends, their friends have added them, and that's it. There's nothing else to do.

Remember the AOF Method from Chapter 2—Activities, Objects, Features? A point from that method bears repeating. Don't simply set up profiles (or any feature) if it doesn't support a primary activity! The three profiles in this section are good examples of profiles that support their primary activity.

Get Out of the Way

Of all the design elements that people use, the profile is the most personal. It is how people express themselves within the world that is your application. When it is core to the experience, tread lightly. A good

---

4   A good article on Friendster's downfall: http://www.nytimes.com/2006/10/15/business/ yourmoney/15friend.html?pagewanted=3

rule of thumb: don't impose too many restrictions on how people can manage their profile, and what information is found there. Simply get out of the way. Designing profiles is about showing what's happening and getting out of the way.

Emphasize the Person's Uniqueness

I vividly remember a day in high school when a teacher pointed out, to the great pleasure of my class, that the "alternative" kids—the mysterious ones wearing black shirts and lots of piercings in places they probably regret now—all looked the same. In their shared nonconformity they were actually conforming *with each other*. Instantly their mysterious aura vanished.

Those kids were like most of us. We like to view ourselves as unique. Even if we're pretty normal, we like to see our contributions as unique and valuable.

Keep this tendency in mind when designing and writing. Be sure to reinforce how unique someone's contributions are or will be. What might they add that others can't? In any given niche, what distinguishes a person as unique?

Netflix.com, a movie-rental-by-mail service, is an excellent place to find uniqueness at work. The goal of their service is to get the best movies into your hands. Part of their strategy to do that is to get people to invest time and energy in rating movies. The more movies people rate, the better Netflix gets at its recommendations.

The Netflix Movies For You screen is built around your unique movie preferences. Each element on the screen is in some way related to which movies you've enjoyed and rated within the system. Netflix makes recommendations based on your history of reviews, so at every turn, they try to get you to give more ratings, which then improves future recommendations. This is personalization at its best, when all a person can see are the elements of their uniqueness.

Figure 5.6 The Netflix Movies for You screen reeks of uniqueness. The success of the service relies almost entirely on recognizing a person's individual movie preferences.

Another interesting use of this technique is on Alistapart.com, which challenges would-be commenters with the question "Got something to say?" This challenges readers to ask themselves what sort of unique contribution they could make.

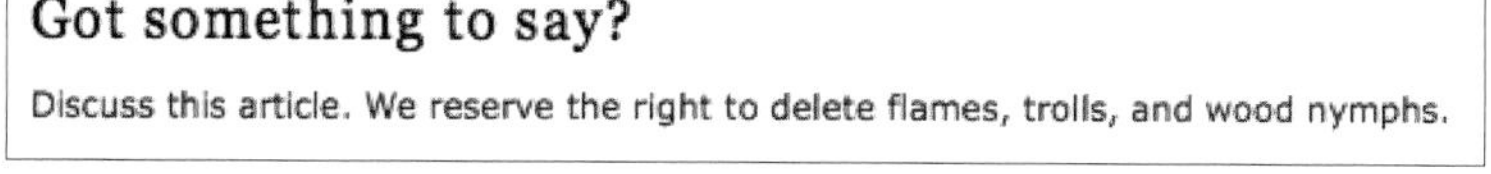

Got something to say?

Discuss this article. We reserve the right to delete flames, trolls, and wood nymphs.

Figure 5.7 The comments section on Alistapart.com emphasizes a person's unique contribution by challenging them.

An Experiment in Uniqueness

Research suggests that uniqueness can have a positive effect on people's willingness to participate. In a 2005 study called "Using social psychology to motivate contributions to online communities,"[5] a research team of twelve social psychologists found that when a person's uniqueness was emphasized on copy in a movie-rating application, they rated more movies.

The way they tested this was by emphasizing uniqueness in periodic emails sent to participants. Some members of the study received emails containing mentions of uniqueness of contribution, while other members didn't. The members who did have uniqueness mentioned ended up contributing more than those who didn't.

This is an important finding, because it suggests ways forward in writing copy and designing flows. For example, we can:

▶ Add uniqueness copy in and around activities that ask for participation

▶ Emphasize that the person is making a positive contribution

▶ Expose what benefit is realized from their unique contribution

▶ Remind people over time of their uniqueness

▶ Create views and flows that show differences between their content and others' content (for example: books I have bought that my friends haven't)

▶ Create screens that highlight the differences between people, thus emphasizing the uniqueness of the individual

Leverage Reciprocity

Reciprocity means exchange for mutual benefit. If you can design an interface to elicit a feeling of reciprocity, people will feel they should contribute because they have benefited from others' previous contributions.

Reciprocity is common on web sites at which you are invited to rate or review items. Someone browsing the vast collection of restaurant reviews at Yelp.com can easily recognize the benefit they are receiving: thousands of people adding their opinion help them make a decision about which restaurant to try.

---

5   For more on this experiment, see http://jcmc.indiana.edu/vol10/issue4/ling.html

According to the "rule" of reciprocity, when this happens, the person feels obligated in some small way to contribute a restaurant review. They realize that others will then in turn benefit from their contribution, just as they have benefited from others.

Yelp does a good job of leveraging reciprocity on their profile pages. Before you have written a profile, they gently nudge you to do so by suggesting that "It's your turn to be the critic." This copy does two things: 1) it suggests that in all fairness (reciprocity-wise) it's your turn to write reviews, and 2) it empowers you to be a food critic, which is a great way to motivate someone. Who *doesn't* want to be a food critic?

Figure 5.8 Yelp does a good job of leveraging reciprocity by hinting that "It's your turn to be the critic."

Sometimes designing for reciprocity simply means giving the opportunity to respond or act in kind. When someone does something like comment on a blog or add as a friend, simply notify the recipient and provide an option to do the same.

LinkedIn really knows how to leverage reciprocity with their "recommendations" feature. When someone writes a recommendation for someone else, there is an urge to return the favor. Browsing the site makes this abundantly clear — many of the recommendations are indeed reciprocated. To elicit this action, LinkedIn can simply give someone who has received a recommendation the opportunity to respond in kind.

"Reid has the ability to quickly distill issues in the board room and offer insight in a way that sticks. His battle tested internet experience and tremendous raw intelligence have been tremendous assets in Kiva's early days. I highly recommend Reid as an angel investor or advisor if you're running a start up internet company. He's acutely aware of entrepreneurial challenges and trade-offs -- there's real wisdom to his counsel." *May 14, 2007*

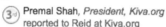 Premal Shah, *President, Kiva.org*
reported to Reid at Kiva.org

"Premal brings all of the skills and abilities of a driven, accomplished silicon valley entrepreneur to the unique organization of Kiva. As an entrepreneur, Premal already has the essential characteristics: smart and analytic, fast and responsive, intelligent risk taking, focus. He applies those essential characteristics to Kiva in that he also understands and cares about the *marketplace* of micro-finance, changing the world through enabling entrepreneurs -- and thus making real sustainable inroads to the problem of poverty. Finally, and not least, he's also a pleasure to work with a second time." *May 18, 2007*

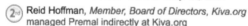 Reid Hoffman, *Member, Board of Directors, Kiva.org*
managed Premal indirectly at Kiva.org

Figure 5.9 LinkedIn's recommendations feature powerfully leverages reciprocity to drive participation.

Allow for Reputation

A person's reputation is the set of beliefs or opinions that others hold about them. We each have a reputation, even if it is a small one. While we can cultivate it, it ultimately has to come from other people. The power of reputation is that it is unbiased, it is the opinion of others.

When reputation works well, people can judge others and their possible interactions accurately. On a social web site, this might mean they decide to go through with a business transaction or take a recommendation about which movie to watch. When reputation doesn't work, a person can't get an accurate impression of another person.

Designing for reputation is about deciding (or discovering) what signals make for a positive reputation within the culture of the community who uses your software. For example, let's imagine you're building a social web application for chefs. Even in two such closely related professions as head chef and prep chef, reputation might be based on different criteria.[6] It is up to you, the designer, to figure out what these criteria are. Head chefs might gain reputation because of the unique ways they can combine flavors or redefine classic dishes. Prep chefs, on the other hand, might gain reputation by how quickly and precisely they can cut food.

The review site Yelp.com has powerful reputation features:

▶ **Number of friends.** In many social web apps, this is an implicit indicator of reputation

▶ **Number of reviews written.** The more the person performs the primary activity on the site, the better their reputation is

▶ **Ratings of reviews written.** How people have judged the reviews you've written: were they useful, funny, or cool?

▶ **Number and quality of comments from other members.** Another generic feature seen on many social apps

▶ **Number of Fans.** A fan is someone who follows your reviews—this is one of the highest compliments one can pay on Yelp

▶ **Number and quality of compliments from other members.** This is more explicit than comments or friends in determining reputation

▶ **Number of Firsts.** Firsts in Yelp are the first reviews of a business. It is a coveted achievement to be the first to review a restaurant on the service

▶ **Member Since.** Reputation is based in part on how long you've been a member of Yelp

▶ **Elite Squad Member.** Members of the Elite Squad have a very positive reputation within the community

Notice that some of the reputation features on Yelp are found on other social web apps (Friends, Fans) while some are specific to the domain (Reviews, Firsts, Elite Squad).

---

6   For an interesting story on the reputations of chefs, check out: http://www.time.com/time/magazine/article/0,9171,428007,00.html

Figure 5.10 Yelp.com is full of both implicit and explicit reputation-based features: number of Friends, Fans, Compliments, number of Firsts, review feedback, and the Elite Squad all signal reputation within the world of Yelp.

It makes sense to do this, because not everyone will be good at garnering reputation in all possible ways. Some people might not have that many friends on the service, for example, but they still could contribute very valuable reviews that get rated highly. Yelp does a great job allowing multiple ways to achieve a positive reputation. This enables more people to gain a reputation for the things they do best.

When Reputation is Crucial to Cooperation

On Yelp, reputation is a nice-to-have. It is not crucial for every transaction, as it is possible to read and write reviews without knowing the reviewer's standing in the Yelp community.

In some cases, like on the auction site eBay, reputation is crucial for cooperation. Buyers and sellers never meet face-to-face, as they do in most purchasing situations. If buyers couldn't effectively judge the reputation of the person they're giving money to, then the transaction wouldn't happen.

eBay works because of a sophisticated reputation system built out of several design elements refined over time. The system is based on what they call a "Feedback Score." When a transaction occurs on eBay, the buyer and seller each leave feedback about the experience. Feedback consists of a rating (positive, negative, or neutral), and a short comment. These ratings are used to determine feedback scores.

Feedback scores are what other people in the system see while they are bidding, so they are a crucial indicator of reputation. If your feedback score is high, then others will trust you and be more likely to do business with you. If your feedback score is low, they're more likely to pass and do business with someone else.

The process goes like this:

▶ After a transaction has occurred, sellers and buyers each rate the transaction by leaving feedback[7]

▶ For every positive feedback rating someone receives, their feedback score rises by one point

▶ For every negative feedback rating someone receives, their feedback score lowers by one point

▶ The buyer's and seller's "feedback profile" is updated to show their cumulative feedback score as well as each individual feedback rating

The "Feedback Profile" is the primary screen showing reputation on eBay. It contains a person's entire feedback history, both as a buyer and a seller. It is a sophisticated document.

Since so much money is changing hands on eBay, members pay tremendous attention to what goes on here. Stories of fraud and gaming the system crop up now and then, but eBay has consistently provided enough of a reputation system to keep it all working. (Of course, it doesn't hurt that they boost this with a visible Fraud Investigation Team).

---

7 Interestingly, in February 2008 eBay decided to remove the ability for sellers to give feedback to buyers

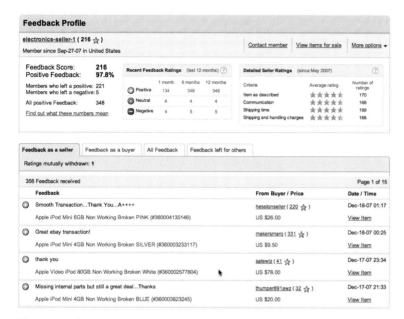

Figure 5.11 eBay's Feedback Profile is a sophisticated document that shows feedback ratings over time. It is a snapshot of reputation within the eBay system.

Some ways that eBay protects your feedback score:

▸ Each feedback rating raises or lowers your total feedback score by one point only—so one bad day or one good day doesn't mean much, what matters is your reputation over the long term

▸ Each member can only affect someone's feedback score by one point— one person cannot have an undue effect on another's score

▸ The comments associated with feedback allow people to describe any outstanding circumstances

▸ eBay shows recent feedback more prominently than older feedback, so what you have done lately is more important

▸ eBay has a very clear section describing in minute detail how reputation works on the site

▸ eBay has sophisticated ways to monitor whether people are pushing up their own feedback scores by creating multiple accounts

The sophistication of this design can be seen in figure 5.12. It is not a system you can build overnight. eBay has slowly refined it over several years.

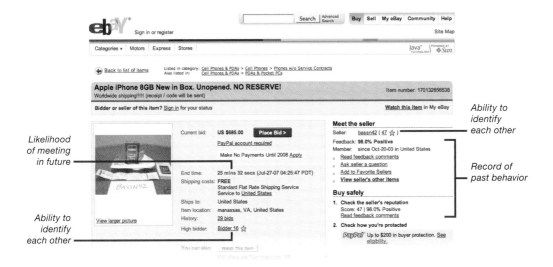

Figure 5.12 eBay has a sophisticated reputation system that is crucial to the site's success.

Promote a Sense of Efficacy

While reputation is what people say about you, efficacy is your own sense that you're being productive. In many cases these two things go hand in hand. The more your reputation grows, the more productive you feel.

A sense of efficacy (pronounced EFF-icka-see) is the feeling you get when you're doing good work, and having an effect on the world around you. Efficacy is an important factor in some people's decision to participate: sometimes they'll only participate if they feel they can make a difference.

Interviews that I've had with people using social software play this out. In one project I interviewed several people who were writing reviews of restaurants. I asked them what motivated them to participate. Though nobody ever said the word *efficacy*, it was clear from their comments that this was so. Here are a few quotes from that research:

> I just want to help others in my situation.
>
> If there's a restaurant that hasn't been reviewed and I think people should know about it, I'll add one.
>
> I don't want people wasting their money on a bad experience (so I write good reviews to prevent that).

Designing for efficacy means focusing on elements that provide feedback to people about how valuable their contribution was.

We've already mentioned the elements of the Yelp profile that help drive reputation. One in particular—compliments—helps to give a strong sense of efficacy as well.

Figure 5.13 Compliments on Yelp.com are aimed at giving people a sense of efficacy—that they're having a positive effect on their environment.

Getting Two People to Cooperate

Robert Axelrod, whose article "The Evolution of Cooperation" (later a book) has become one of the most cited articles in the history of *Science* magazine, identifies three requirements for the possibility of cooperation.[8] Interestingly, Axelrod wasn't using the web for his research, as it didn't exist. He was observing people in the flesh. His observations, however, apply very well on sites like eBay.com, where cooperation is critical.

1. **Probability of Meeting in the Future.** If there is no or low probability of meeting in the future, then there is little incentive to act nicely. Either person can easily act selfishly and get away with it because they won't have to deal with seeing the other person again. Online, making sure two people meet in the future can be difficult to achieve, usually meaning that both parties will continue using the service (as they never actually see each other in the flesh).

   On eBay, the place where two people meet is at the end of the auction, when the seller ships an item to the buyer to complete the actual transaction.

2. **Ability to Identify Each Other.** As the famous *New Yorker* cartoon said, "On the Internet, nobody knows you're a dog." On eBay, surprisingly, you never really know who you're dealing with. But their reputation system is so sophisticated that you don't need to. All you need to know is someone's reputation within the system. You don't need to know their real name, just their eBay handle. The proof is in the pudding: a simple handle is all that is necessary to transact billions of dollars

3. **Record of Past Behavior.** The best way to predict the future is to look at the past. We all have some sense of the truth of this. eBay is fantastic at showing a history of past behavior on both the item page as well as the Feedback Profile.

---

8   "The Evolution of Cooperation": http://www.sciencemag.org/cgi/content/abstract/211/4489/1390

Provide a Sense of Control

Providing a sense of control is crucial in the design of social web sites. The social network site Facebook learned this lesson the hard way in early September 2006. Their experience is a casebook study.

At that time Facebook released a new feature called the news feed and a similar feature, the mini feed. Like all social web apps, Facebook was trying to increase the social interaction of the site.

The news feed was meant to show participants more information about what was going on around them. It was located on the home page (when people are logged in) and showed people all the latest activity of their friends. It showed when someone added a friend, when someone joined a group, and when someone wrote a message on another's profile. This information was not new. Anybody could find it out by visiting each of their friends' profiles in turn. The primary innovation of the news feed was that it aggregated formerly isolated information in one, easy-to-read screen.

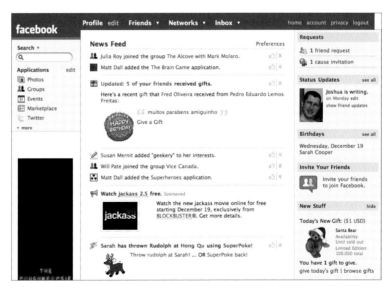

Figure 5.14 Facebook's news feed was meant to simply display more of what was going on. The people who first saw it, however, didn't like that.

Within twenty-four hours of release, however, the Facebook community revolted loudly against the new features. They claimed it was a violation of their privacy. Within hours, a new group was created on

Facebook to denounce this feature. It was called "Students Against the Facebook News Feed" (Facebook hadn't yet opened up the service to all). The group quickly gained steam, gathering hundreds of thousands of members within just days of its formation. It was clear that Facebook had to do something.

Figure 5.15 The protest group "Students Against Facebook News Feed" was created and grew within the very framework it was protesting.

Mark Zuckerberg, the twenty-two-year-old CEO of Facebook, had a response for them. He wrote a blog post telling everyone to "calm down," pointing out that the feature didn't expose anything that wasn't already on the site. He said that it was Facebook's highest priority to protect its members, and pointed out that none of the information on the news feed features was actually new. The only difference was that now all that information had been aggregated into one place.

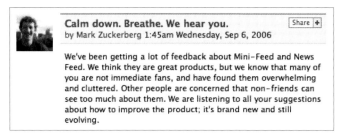

Figure 5.16 Mark Zuckerberg's first attempt at calming down the masses during the news feed blowup. Telling people to "calm down" while not addressing their concerns is not a good idea...

If you read Zuckerberg's post closely, you'll notice that he doesn't really acknowledge the issue at hand: the *feeling* that privacy had been invaded. What he does instead is try to rationalize the feature by pointing out that it doesn't show any more information than people could have found themselves.

Of course, that wasn't good enough. People were still angry. The Facebook community didn't appreciate Zuckerberg telling them what they should or should not get excited about. Some compared the news feed to putting up a video camera outside your living room window. After all, anybody could see in if they happened to be walking by. This would simply be an aggregated view for everyone else. No new information, just like the news feed. So the protest group grew in force. Instead of quieting the problem, Zuckerberg's comments had made the situation worse.

Facebook tried again, and their next attempt to quell the uprising worked. First, Zuckerberg finally apologized. Second, Facebook added privacy options for the news feed that allowed people to turn off the features. Within a couple days of the apology and new privacy settings, the uproar had blown over.

The Real Issue: a Sense of Control

The afterstory might be as telling as the uprising. Even though hundreds of thousands of people joined the protest group, only a small percentage of Facebook members ever changed their privacy settings! Most people leave the default (no privacy) setting intact. So even though they protested the new feature on the basis of a lack of privacy, it was really control they sought.

As noted security expert Bruce Schneier explained, privacy is more about control than it is about secrecy. Once Facebook put in controls that allowed people to choose what information was published, they were satisfied:

> Welcome to the complicated and confusing world of privacy in the information age. Facebook didn't think there would be any problem; all it did was take available data and aggregate it in a novel way for what it perceived was its customers' benefit. Facebook members instinctively understood that making this information easier to display was an enormous difference, and that privacy is more about control than about secrecy.[9]

---

9   http://www.wired.com/politics/security/commentary/securitymatters/2006/09/71815

Confer Ownership

The mere name MySpace confers a sense of ownership. It has its audience thinking: this is my online space. I own it. I can do with it what I want. YouTube takes the other tack, using the word "you" instead of "me," but the result is the same. It's yours, you own it, do with it what you want.

Both sites confer ownership to their audience. They make it clear that this space is their property. Using words like "my" or "your" may seem like little more than rhetoric, but there's real psychology at play here. These sites are leveraging what's called the *Endowment Effect*.[10] The Endowment Effect is the tendency of people to value things more once a sense of ownership has been established.

It's not just about site names, however. In design, ownership can be conveyed best in copywriting and labeling. By using words such as "you" and "my" where appropriate, designers can imply ownership and give people the feeling that their content is something worth holding onto.

Conferring ownership has several benefits:

▸ Leverages the Endowment Effect to make content seem more valuable

▸ Conveys a sense of responsibility for the content if others are around (people will be more likely to take care of it)

▸ Empowers people by suggesting that they are in control of their content

▸ Makes the site feel more familiar and friendly

One of the oldest and best examples of this is Amazon. They go further than most apps, even conferring ownership of an entire portion of the site to each person who has an account. When I go to Amazon, there is a section called "Joshua's Amazon.com." Not only did they give me ownership of content, I even have my own version of Amazon.com!

Figure 5.17 Amazon.com confers ownership in a big way. In this sliver of screen alone, there are seven references to things that are mine.

---

10 http://en.wikipedia.org/wiki/Endowment_effect

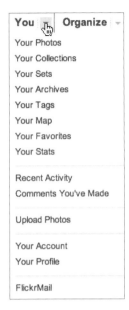

Figure 5.18 The photo-sharing site Flickr really knows how to confer ownership to its members. Their navigation is all about YOU.

Flickr.com also does a great job of conferring ownership. They sprinkle the site with ownership words, making it absolutely clear whose content we're dealing with.

In Flickr's navigation scheme, for example, one of the tabs is labeled "You." When you click on the dropdown for this tab, you get fourteen options, eleven of which refer to content that is "yours." Flickr's labels make it very clear who owns what on the site.

Don't take conveying ownership too far, however. The designers at Motortopia, a motor-enthusiast site, designed a panel on their profile pages that is jarring because of an over-emphasis on ownership. Instead of focusing on the person who is *using* the app, they display over and over the username of the person whose profile one is looking at. In this case, it would be safer to go without the repeated username. In general, other people's ownership is implicit on a profile page and doesn't need to be emphasized. Instead, emphasize ownership to the person using the app.

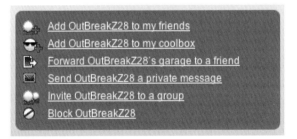

Figure 5.19 Motortopia.com took ownership a bit too far, making each option hard to scan. In this case, it would be much easier to read without the username.

Show Desired Behavior

If you peruse the profiles found on many of the pages of Yelp, you might come away thinking that you've been transported to Lake Wobegon where "all the children are above average."

That's because Yelp takes pains to promote certain profiles whose owners behave as model citizens. They tend to have huge numbers of friends, lots of reviews, and other gaudy numbers that represent success on the site. It's clear that the designers at Yelp want to promote desired behavior in the hopes that others would see and emulate it.

For example, on its homepage Yelp places a "review of the day." Invariably, the review is written by a reputable member of Yelp who has amazing profile numbers. When newcomers see this review, they learn what behavior is appreciated. They learn by observing what happens.

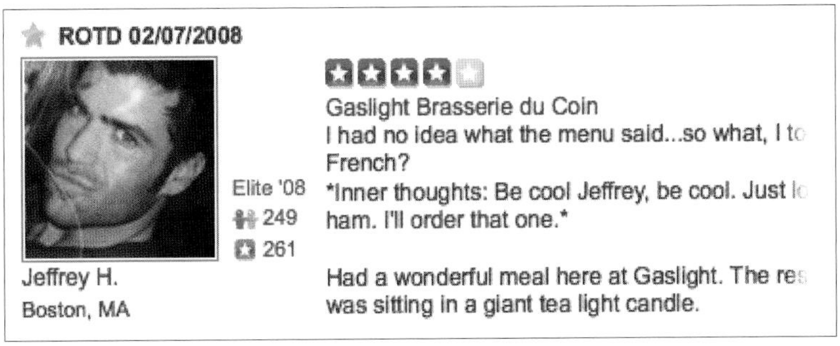

⭐ **ROTD 02/07/2008**

Jeffrey H.
Boston, MA

Elite '08
👥 249
🗓 261

⭐⭐⭐⭐☐
Gaslight Brasserie du Coin
I had no idea what the menu said...so what, I to French?
Inner thoughts: Be cool Jeffrey, be cool. Just lo ham. I'll order that one.

Had a wonderful meal here at Gaslight. The res was sitting in a giant tea light candle.

Figure 5.20 Yelp.com places "reviews of the day" in prominent locations to show desired behavior to newcomers. They tend to have impressive numbers that show successful behavior to others.

Endowment Effect

The Endowment Effect is the idea that people value something more when they feel a sense of ownership. We all know what this is like. From the moment we first compare our bicycles with our friends' bikes, there's something special about ours simply because it is ours.

The classic study of the endowment effect involves economics. To test for the presence of the effect, researchers usually test whether or not people will insist upon selling an item for more than they can buy it for. This would show that they value it more because they own it.

This quickly gets murky, however, because there are many shades of "ownership." Technically, we own something the moment we pay money for it. But for many things, this notion of ownership is weak. Certainly, we give items meaning based on our history with them. We value a gift from a loved one much more than the exact same item received in some other way.

From a less economic point of view, however, we have a very common way to describe the Endowment Effect. When we say that an item has "sentimental value," suggesting that its value goes beyond its inherent value as an object, we are pointing to the Endowment Effect.

On the web, we're often talking not just about items we own, but items we create. This is important because items that we create (pictures, blog posts, bookmarks, comments, etc.) tend to have much more meaning than items we did not create. Everyone likes to feel ownership in and be proud of their creations.

Attachment to a Group

Attachment to a group is one of the more straightforward reasons why people participate online. You can find a lot of people interested in the same weird things you are!

Yahoo, Google, and MSN Groups are applications dedicated to supporting groups. They are massive. Each service has millions of members who create groups on nearly all topics known to mankind, from cricket fans to stupid joke buffs to alternative medicine consumers.

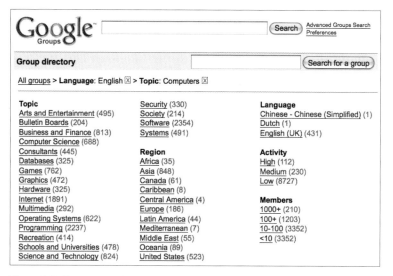

Figure 5.21 The number of groups within the computers category is astounding. Pretty much every topic imaginable is covered.

Of course, you don't need to use "group" software to be part of a group online. Groups are really the center of most social software.

Fun Features

Last but not least, a major reason why people participate is simply because it's fun. Web applications run the gamut of fun, from cold, process-based apps that are no fun at all, to productivity-sucking games that are nothing but fun.

Fun isn't just fun, though. Creating fun web apps can be a great way to get people engaged, even in serious activities. The site Social Impact Games[11] is a compendium of such games, chronicling apps that exist to have fun as well as teach us something along the way.

The folks at Twitter know how to add fun to their social web application. For Valentine's Day 2008, they added functionality that let someone declare their love for someone else.

Figure 5.22 The folks at Twitter created a tiny little addition to the app that made Valentine's Day a little more fun for everyone.

Figure 5.23 What Twitter output when you typed in the code above.

In Search of Passion

Once you have a number of people who use your web site on an ongoing basis, your hope is to get at least a few of them to become passionate users. It's these people who then support new people interested in your service and are always telling everyone how wonderful you are.

Figure 5.24 The hurdle of emotional attachment (passionate use) won't be cleared by everybody. But tilt the odds in your favor by *being passionate* in order to receive passion in return.

Truthfully, if there were an easy way to create emotional attachment, there would be many more passionate users out there. Kathy Sierra, who writes the Creating Passionate Users blog,[12] says a big part this last hurdle is about helping your users *learn*. If you can help people learn about their world (and assuming your software makes sense in that world) then you empower them to see themselves in a better light. They literally feel better about themselves. Kathy calls this moment of self-empowerment "users kicking ass".

Viewed in this way, the major hurdle to passionate use is not only reached after a person is using your software regularly, but can be seeded much earlier, when they are first learning about your software. As I mentioned in Chapter 3, an authentic conversation is the start to any strong relationship. In short, passion works both ways. You need to exude it in order to receive it in return.

Conclusion

The design of social web applications rests on our ability to identify and support the basic motivations of the people who use our software. Once we identify what those motivations are, we can fine-tune our design appropriately.

The basic motivations outlined in this chapter—identity, uniqueness, reciprocity, reputation, efficacy, control, ownership, attachment to a group, and fun—are all possible reasons for someone to use your software. Your web site will most likely draw upon a unique mixture of these motivations. In some cases, your users will even become passionate about your software. You can make this possible by helping people learn and by being passionate yourself.

Finally, these basic motivations for online participation apply to a wide variety of web sites. In the next chapter we'll look more closely at a particularly interesting type of web site: those that harness collective intelligence.

---

12 http://headrush.typepad.com

Design for Collective Intelligence

The wonderful world of complex, adaptive systems

"When working in social, economic, environmental systems, we often assume one action has one result that it will happen relatively soon.

But experience has shown us that we are managing tightly interconnected, delayed, complex systems where one action has multiple, often counterintuitive, results. Delays and perverse effects are common.

Our brains just don't capture these system features well."

—Sustainability Institute[1]

---

1 Sustainability Institute: http://www.sustainer.org

It's not often you hear of a web site *dropping* a feature. In a world of rampant feature creep, we hear press releases and blog reports daily about our favorite services adding new, better features. It's incredibly rare that a fully-released feature is taken *out* of a web site.

Yet dropping a feature is exactly what the designers at Digg.com did on February 1, 2007. Digg is a social news site that collects stories submitted by users and provides a voting mechanism by which people can *digg* those stories. When stories enter the Digg system, they're displayed on the Upcoming page. The more diggs a story gets (the most *dugg* stories), the more prominent its placement on the site. This is called getting promoted. If a story gets enough diggs, it is promoted to the venerable Digg home page, where tens of thousands of visitors will see it over the course of a few hours. If a story gets submitted but fails to garner enough diggs, it simply disappears from the Digg site after a short time.

The feature the designers at Digg dropped was the Top Diggers page, which displayed the people (*diggers*) who were most successful at getting stories promoted to the home page.

	Username	Popular ▼	Submitted	Popular Ratio	Dugg	Comments	Profile Views
1	digitalgopher	988	2049	48 %	11781	658	95,635
2	p9s50W5k4GUD2c6	752	1484	51 %	14405	1127	54,137
3	CLIFFosakaJAPAN	750	5993	13 %	8335	875	58,582
4	qwc	668	1989	34 %	23588	1389	41,962
5	supernova17	608	1301	47 %	35288	1359	55,723
6	MrBabyMan	561	3224	17 %	11766	990	27,954
7	bonlebon	552	4952	11 %	17200	2020	60,971
8	chrisek	546	1583	34 %	27261	70	23,126
9	BloodJunkie	524	1719	30 %	15977	2422	39,625
10	webtech	509	950	54 %	38296	256	36,796

Figure 6.1 Top Diggers page on digg.com. In February 2007, Digg actually dropped this page from the site, citing concerns over manipulating the popular stories on the site.

Digg CEO Kevin Rose explains the reason for dropping the feature:

> (We've noticed) a disappointing trend... over the past several months. Some of our top users... are being blamed by some outlets as leading efforts to manipulate Digg. These users have been listed on the "Top Diggers" area of the site that was created in the early days of Digg.... The list served a great purpose of recognizing those who were working hard to make Digg a great site, as well as a way for new users to discover new content. Now... we believe there are better ways to discover new friends based on your interests and what you're digging.

So what does this all mean? After considerable internal debate and discussion with many of those who make up the Top Digger list, we've decided to remove the list beginning tomorrow.[2]

As Rose hints, the situation that led to the decision to remove the Top Diggers feature from Digg wasn't a single incident, but arose from the complex interaction of many people over time. Digg made a social design decision that affected not only the people on the list and those who voiced concerns, but everyone on the Digg site.

This issue is unique to social software: sometimes it makes sense to focus design decisions on the good of the group at the expense of the individual.

When Digg took away the Top Diggers feature, they made the system less valuable for the Top Diggers but more valuable for the larger Digg community over the long term.

Complex Adaptive Systems

Digg, like many other interesting things in life—ant colonies, immune systems, ecosystems, politics, economics, science—is what is known in academic fields as a *complex system*. A complex system is "a system composed of interconnected parts that as a whole exhibit one or more properties (behavior among the possible properties) not obvious from the properties of the individual parts."[3] The interactions of the Top Diggers, and the reactions of the others on the site, are an example of this complexity.

In addition to being complex, some complex systems are also adaptive, meaning that they have the capacity to change over time. This trait is very important to their survival. Digg adapts is through the digging feature. If enough people digg new stories, the system adapts to give them more time on the site. If people don't digg them enough, the system replaces them with newer ones, sometimes in as little as one hour.[4]

Additionally, the needs of these systems change over time. While the Top Diggers feature was good for a small, growing Digg, it was not so good for a larger, established Digg community. Thus these systems are, for the designers tasked with keeping them healthy, a moving target.

---

2   http://blog.digg.com/?p=60

3   http://en.wikipedia.org/wiki/Complex_system

4   Francis Wu and Bernardo Huberman study this stuff: http://technology.newscientist.com/article/dn11702-diggcom-reveals-news-stories-fade-after-1-hour.html

Complex Systems Everywhere!

Digg is merely one of many sites that are complex adaptive systems. Consider popular web destinations that similarly aggregate behavior.

- ▶ **Amazon** aggregates the collective opinion of the people reading product reviews to determine which reviews are helpful.

- ▶ **Google** aggregates the collective opinion of people who create and link to web pages, assessing where to display pages in results.

- ▶ **Netflix** aggregates the collective ratings of millions of movie fans to provide better movie recommendations.

- ▶ **Wikipedia** aggregates the collective knowledge of its editors to provide a single, authoritative encyclopedia.

- ▶ **eBay** aggregates the collective feedback of buyers to provide seller ratings that influence whether a deal goes through or not.

Collective Intelligence

The goal of many of these complex systems is the same: to aggregate the individual actions of many people in order to surface the best or most relevant content. The intelligence that emerges from this activity is often called *collective intelligence*.[5]

Collective intelligence is based on the idea that by aggregating the behavior of many people, we can gain novel insights.

How Complex Adaptive Systems Work

Digg and other aggregation systems rely on the fact that while no individual is right all the time, in the collective a large number of users can be amazingly accurate in their decisions and choices. Amazon, Digg, Google, Netflix, and many other sites base their recommendations of products, news, sites, movies, etc., on aggregated opinion.

To do this, the sites record the actions of all the people using the system and look for patterns in that behavior. Where patterns emerge, intelligence arises. In general, this can be described as a three-step process:

- ▶ **Initial Action.** Content is submitted into the system. On Digg, this happens when someone submits a story. On Amazon, it happens when someone writes a product review. From here, the life of the content is outside of the submitter's hands, as its fate is determined by the rules of the system and its interaction with other people.

---

5   http://en.wikipedia.org/wiki/Collective_intelligence

▸ **Display.** The content is displayed for others to see and act on. How each site displays content depends on the goals of the site, including time of submission, rate of other submissions, as well as various algorithms that predetermine relevancy. The display changes over time as more content is introduced, which is one of the hallmarks of adaptive systems.

▸ **Feedback.** The people using the system are given an opportunity to provide feedback on the content to assess its quality. They can provide positive feedback to signal good content, or negative feedback to signal bad content. The system then adjusts and redisplays the content, starting a feedback loop. This feedback loop continues and the content can either rise to the top, stabilize in some way, lose its novelty and drop off, or get removed if deemed inappropriate.

The following table illustrates different forms of the three steps for many popular social systems.

	Action	Display	Feedback
Digg	Submitting a news story	Upcoming, popular, homepage	Digg, share, and bury stories
Amazon	Writing a product review	Mostful, most recent	Is this Helpful? Report this, Comment
Netflix	Rating a movie	Recommended movies	Add to queue, Rate movie, Not interested
Google	Writing a web page	Results based on relevancy	Link between web pages, Click on search results
Wikipedia	Starting an article	Article page	Edit articles over time
Del.icio.us	Saving & tagging a bookmark	Most popular, Related tags, all tags	Copy bookmarks
Flickr	Uploading and tagging a picture	Interestingness, popularity, clusters	Tagging, setting Favorites
YouTube	Uploading a video	YouTube interface, embedded in blogs	Favorite it, Report it, Embed it

Initial Action

The first step in an adaptive system occurs when people add content to it. Adaptive social systems need a constant supply of fresh content to maintain the interest of their users. However, the rate of flow of new content must be regulated carefully, or else too much content vies for people's limited attention.

We are all too familiar with the pain of wading through a basically unrestricted flow of content. The email system, which makes sending content effortless and essentially free, is nearly overwhelmed with SPAM. Systems need a way to control the influx of content.

Barriers to Entry

A hurdle that prevents participation is called a *barrier to entry*. Barriers to entry are commonly described as beneficial in the business world, as they keep competitors from entering a market. In the social software world, the removal or creation of barriers to entry is crucial to the overall health of the system.

Derek Powazek, who wrote the book *Design for Community*,[6] notes that "all communities are exclusionary to some degree." He distinguishes between three types of barriers to entry:

▸ **Informal barriers**. Informal barriers are those that exclude subtly, such as design with an aesthetic that attracts a certain type of person, or copywriting that speaks to a specific audience.

▸ **Formal barriers**. Formal barriers to entry are things that exclude blatantly, like requiring an account, requiring certain software, or any planned measure that restricts participation.

▸ **Extreme barriers**. Extreme barriers are those that create exclusivity by only allowing certain people in. The invitation-only social network asmallworld.com, which caters to the rich and famous, is a good example of an extreme barrier to entry.

On Digg, like on many social sites, you need an account to submit stories. Then, the process of submitting stories has two steps.

The first step is to enter the link you're submitting. This is a normal URL. You also choose the type of content it is: a news story, image, or video. Digg helps people by providing a nice set of guidelines.

After you click "Continue" in step 1, Digg takes a moment to analyze the link to see if it's a duplicate. This helps keep the system clean. When Digg thinks you've submitted duplicate content, it notifies you that the story has already been submitted.

---

6   Powazek, Derek, *Design for Community*. New Riders, 2006.

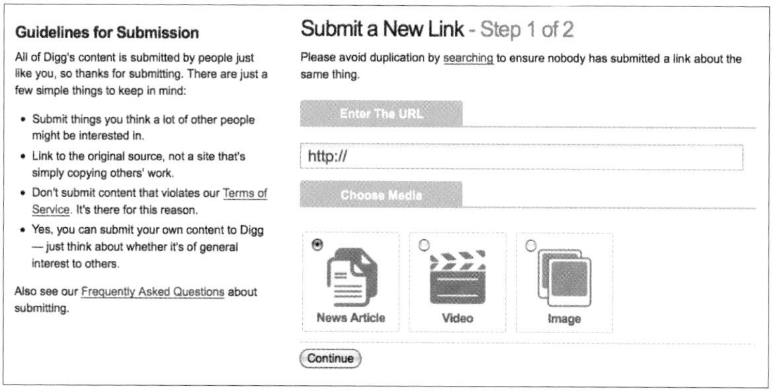

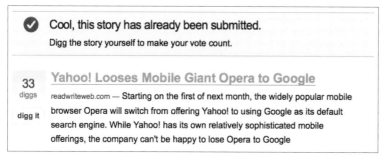

Figure 6.2 The first step in submitting content to digg.com. The helpful submission guidelines head off problems before they occur.

Figure 6.3 Digg checks to makes sure that your submission isn't a duplicate. This keeps redundant content out of the system.

If the submission is not a duplicate, Digg analyzes the page and grabs any relevant content from it, including the page title, a description, and any images in the page. It then allows you to choose which elements are appropriate as part of your submission. This step makes it much easier to digg content, as you don't have to do any heavy lifting of grabbing the content yourself.

Finally, Digg adds a check to make sure that the submitter of content is indeed a human being.

The initial action on Digg is a crucial step in the system. It determines what content is allowed, makes sure the content is unique, adds data that supports the story, and determines who can and cannot submit content. These decisions act as a barrier to entry to the rest of the system. The quality of content that receives entry into the Digg system depends on the checks at this stage.

Figure 6.4 Step 2 of the Digg submission process makes it easy to customize a submission yet verifies that the submitter is a person.

Other Examples of Initial Action

Adaptive systems do checks on the initial action in many different ways:

▶ **Techmeme** is a news site that aggregates the current news from blogs and other news sources. It started by sourcing its content from a small, core set of blogs, prioritizing their content over the content of others. At present, it sources its content from a larger corpus of sources, but still allows for the serendipity of unknown blogs to appear in its pages.

▶ **Yahoo Buzz** also aggregates news, but uses a group of select publishers as content providers, keeping the number of sources who can add content relatively low. By using only trusted sources, Yahoo keeps quality high, but doesn't have the serendipity of Techmeme.

▶ **Google Search** indexes everything on the web, which makes their initial sample of content extremely large, before they determine the value of that content by studying the interconnectedness among the pages.

▶ **Amazon** moderates customer reviews to make sure that they are relevant and on-topic, weeding out overly promotional and machine-generated reviews. This keeps the content in the system relevant.

Adding Tags

Some services allow people to tag content, which allows aggregation of the content in additional, helpful ways. For example, the social bookmarking site Del.icio.us lets you add tags to bookmarks as you enter them into the system.

del.icio.us / bokardo /	by Joshua Porter	popular | recent
your bookmarks | your network | subscriptions | links for you (9) | post	logged in as **bokardo** | settings | logout | help	

url http://www.businessweek.com/the_thread/techbeat/archives/2008/03/apples_design_p.htm ☐ do not share

description Tech Beat Apple's design process – BusinessWeek

notes This article talks about some of the details of Apples' design process, including using super-high-fidelity mockups.

tags apple businessweek   space separated

(save)

Figure 6.5 Del.icio.us allows people to tag bookmarks as they enter them into the system. This allows the site to aggregate and display tags in helpful ways.

Preprocessing Content Before Display

All content in a system is not equal. Some content may come from authoritative sources, while other content might come from suspect sources. For example, since Google indexes the entire web, it is important for them to analyze where the content comes from to try to determine what is relevant and what is not. Otherwise, sites built by spammers could potentially have as much authority as honest sites.

Not all sites do preprocessing like this. Digg and Amazon simply accept all new content as equal. It doesn't matter who wrote the review on Amazon, or who submitted a story on Digg, it will be added just the same way as usual.

Aggregate Display

The display of content is crucial to how people interact with it. If content is displayed prominently then people will consider it more important. Content displayed less prominently will be considered less important.

In general, content is deemed more important when it is displayed:

- **On a home page**. The home page is visited the most of any page, and therefore it garners the most attention from both site owners and readers.
- **More often**. The more content is displayed and repeated, the more it is considered valuable.
- **At the top of a page**. Just like on the front of a newspaper, above the fold is the prime real estate. The top of a web page is where the most important content is placed online.
- **Higher in ranked displays**. When content is ranked, such as in a "most emailed" list, the content at the top is deemed most valuable.

When content first gets added to an adaptive system, it is usually displayed in an appropriately less prominent location. Digg, for example, has what they call an Upcoming page, which displays all new submissions into the system in reverse-chronological order. These freshly-submitted stories stay on the upcoming page a short period of time, getting pushed off in favor of even fresher content. The Upcoming page is crucial to the functioning of the Digg site because it forces each story to gain its own popularity.

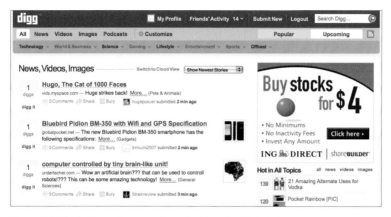

Figure 6.6 Digg's Upcoming page shows freshly-submitted stories.

All of these stories aspire to reach the Digg home page, the ultimate place for grabbing attention, where they will be seen by thousands of people in a very short period of time. In fact, the burst of attention resulting from being on the Digg homepage often makes sites unreachable. So many people visit the site from Digg that the web server is overwhelmed and either slows to a crawl or breaks outright.

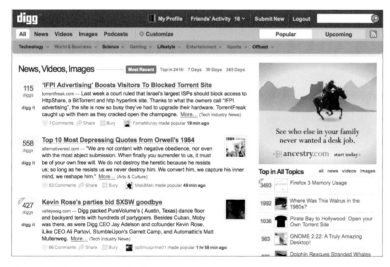

Figure 6.7 The venerable Digg homepage.

Types of Aggregation Ordering

Adaptive systems aggregate content in order to display it back to people. Each service drives engagement with its own combination of ordering that ensures their content is relevant and compelling to the audience. Here are a few of the more popular ways to do this:

- ▶ **Chronological listing**. When items are first added to Digg, they are simply listed by the order in which they are added.

- ▶ **Popularity within a time range**. Del.icio.us simply counts the number of bookmarks that people have saved in the last x hours and orders them from most popular to least popular, displaying as a "most popular" list of bookmarks that people have saved recently[7].

- ▶ **Participant ranking**. The Digg Top Diggers page was a ranking system that took into account measures of desired behavior to come up with an overall rank for each Digger.

- ▶ **Collaborative filtering**. Netflix's recommendation system relies on collaborative filtering to display recommended movies based on your previous ratings.

- ▶ **Relevance**. Services like Google rely on a complex algorithm to determine what to display. Figuring out which content is relevant is a big deal to Google—it's the core value of the entire service.

- ▶ **Social**. Social network sites like Slideshare and Flickr display content based on who it is from. They provide tools for users to indicate which other participants are interesting to them, then adapt the content display based on those connections.

- ▶ **User-based views.** Collaborative sites such as PublicSquare and Goplan set aside a special area to display each user's content back to them so they can see how their content has been acted upon by others, allowing them to orient themselves and begin work.

Display and Social Influence

Why is ordering so important? The obvious reason is that it makes your site easier and more pleasurable to use. But there is a less obvious reason: it communicates to your users what you value. A news site values freshness, a search engine values relevance, a social site values relationships. If you know your site's goals, ordering choices can channel movement toward those goals for user and site owner alike.

---

7   Del.icio.us Most Popular page: http://del.icio.us/popular/

As I mentioned in Chapter 1, The Rise of the Social Web, the interface is the environment in which people live while using your software. It is their world. Most of their behaviors are dictated by the possibilities of interaction that exist there.

The social aspects of the software environment affect our behavior as well. Three sociologists, Duncan Watts, Matthew Salganik, and Peter Dodds, did a study[8] on the effect of social influence in software interfaces, trying to answer the question: how much are we affected by the actions of others?

The MusicLab Study

As part of the research, Watts and colleagues built a web application called MusicLab. MusicLab had a simple interface that allowed people to listen to music and download the songs they liked. As the group downloaded music over time, the download total for each song was calculated.

The key variable in the study was the information shown to users. The researchers created two conditions, one called "independent" and the other called "social influence." Each person who participated in the study was randomly assigned one of the conditions. The people in the "independent" group were shown screens with song information only—the artist and title of the song. This meant that they could not see any evidence of how many people downloaded the songs.

The people assigned to the "social influence" condition were also shown download information. They could easily see the number of downloads people were making of each song. This was the "influence" factor that the researchers were trying to study.

As expected, this additional information had a strong effect on the behavior of the "social influence" group. When download information was included in the interface, people downloaded those songs which had higher download numbers. Given what we know about social proof, as we talked about in Chapter 5, Design for Ongoing Participation, this was to be expected.

But what wasn't expected was how unpredictable the song downloaders were. In order to see if quality always rises to the top, the researchers ran not one but eight "social influence" groups in order to compare the

---

8   See http://www.princeton.edu/~mjs3/musiclab.shtml for full results of the study.

results. If the quality of songs was real, and could be measured consistently, then the same songs should have been downloaded the most in each of the eight groups.

	# of down loads	[Help] [Log off]		# of down loads		# of down loads
HARTSFIELD: "enough is enough"	20	GO MORDECAI: "it does what its told"	12	UNDO: "while the world passes"		24
DEEP ENOUGH TO DIE: "for the sky"	17	PARKER THEORY: "she said"	47	UP FOR NOTHING: "in sight of"		13
THE THRIFT SYNDICATE: "2003 a tragedy"	20	MISS OCTOBER: "pink agression"	27	SILVERFOX: "gnaw"		17
THE BROKEN PROMISE: "the end in friend"	19	POST BREAK TRAGEDY: "florence"	14	STRANGER: "one drop"		10
THIS NEW DAWN: "the belief above the answer"	12	FORTHFADING: "fear"	24	FAR FROM KNOWN: "route 9"		18
NOONER AT NINE: "walk away"	6	THE CALEFACTION: "trapped in an orange peel"	20	STUNT MONKEY: "inside out"		46
MORAL HAZARD: "waste of my life"	8	52METRO: "lockdown"	17	DANTE: "life's mystery"		14
NOT FOR SCHOLARS: "as seasons change"	27	SIMPLY WAITING: "went with the count"	16	FADING THROUGH: "wish me luck"		10

Figure 6.8 The interface shown to the "social influence" group included not only song information, but information about how many other people downloaded the song.

But the study proved this idea false. While songs that did well in one group usually did well in other groups, their rank within each group varied widely. A song that was downloaded the most in one group would be downloaded only an average amount in another group. This

What the MusicLab Study Found

1. The degree of song popularity in the social influence group was substantially higher than in the independent group. The aggregate download data convinced more people that a song was worth downloading than relying on their own independent judgment.

2. The popular songs in the eight social influence groups were not the same! Early download leaders continued to lead not just because they were good songs, but because their visible popularity led to more downloads.

3. The independent group was considered the test for quality, because everybody voted independently with no social influence.

4. The social influence group was influenced much more by the number of downloads than by the quality of the songs.

In the controlled environment of the MusicLab study, the interface meant everything. When social influence was displayed in the interface, songs were downloaded more. Merely knowing what other people are doing changes our behavior.

suggests that the songs that got out to an early lead kept their lead, and that meant more to the final download numbers than the actual quality of the song.

Feedback

Adaptive systems are dependent on feedback to provide value. Feedback is the process of signaling back into the system something that was previously output.

Implicit and Explicit Feedback

Typically a combination of implicit and explicit feedback is used to create a picture of popularity. For example, Amazon's bestseller list (based on implicit feedback) also shows ratings (based on explicit feedback).[9]

Implicit feedback is based on user behavior that is captured while someone moves through a site. Examples include downloading, bookmarking and purchasing.

Explicit feedback comes from someone's explictly-declared preferences, including ratings, reviews, and comments. While this sort of feedback tends to be more accurate in reflecting user taste, it also requires more work from the user and so less data can be collected.

Positive and Negative Feedback

Digg was built around the feedback mechanism. Digg's feedback system consists of two different ways to signal to the system.

When people see a story they like, they digg it, which tells the system that they liked the content. This is a form of positive feedback. When people see a story they don't like, or think is bad in some way (e.g. over-promotional), they bury it, which tells the system that they didn't like the content. This is a form of negative feedback.

Make Feedback Easy

As I noted above, if a particular story gets enough diggs, it gets promoted in the display. Digg gathers this feedback with the "digg it" button shown in figure 6.9.

252
diggs

digg it

Figure 6.9 The Digg widget is the catalyst that drives the site. Digg uses an small widget to make it super-simple to give positive feedback for stories. Users simply click "digg it" and the widget is updated with their vote.

---

9   http://www.amazon.com/gp/bestsellers/dvd/ref=sv_d_3/002-9185630-6136816.

260
diggs

dugg!

Figure 6.10 The after-state of digging. The number of diggs is updated without a reload of the page.

The designers at Digg have made the process of digging incredibly simple. They provide an small AJAX widget that, upon being clicked, immediately updates to show the new number of total diggs.

In former versions of the site, Digg used a non-AJAX approach that required the entire page to be reloaded when someone dugg a story.

Changing to the AJAX widget made a huge difference in participation. Kevin Rose explains:

> When we made the move to the one-click Digg, activity went through the roof. It was just insane! Just the ease of the one-click and you're done made all the difference in the world.[10]

In addition to digging a story, Diggers can voice their displeasure at content as well by burying it. This is the opposite of being dugg. When enough people click "bury it," a story gets demoted until it is actually taken off the site.

On some sites, like Amazon and Craigslist, you can flag content as inappropriate by "reporting" it. This is subtly different than burying it. By reporting it, you signal to the system that you feel the content doesn't belong on the site. This is not necessarily a statement of quality, but one of appropriateness.

Leverage Points

> Give me a big enough lever, and I can move the world.
>
> —Archimedes

Unlike a static site where the designer directly controls every aspect of the content and presentation, an adaptive site is a collaborative effort between the designer and the people who use the site.

Thus the choosing and prioritization of content, which used to be the role of an editor, is now firmly in the hands of the audience. Instead of designing interfaces to reveal editorial direction, designers are now tasked with creating a tool that empowers people to provide feedback into the system, thus helping to direct the presentation of the site themselves.

In creating these tools, we have to consider the dynamics of the relationship between the people and the site, and by identifying leverage points we can gradually fine-tune that relationship.

---

10 http://www.lukew.com/ff/entry.asp?658

Once you identify these leverage points, as I have illustrated by focusing on Digg in figure 6.11, you can optimize them to design healthier systems that enable more vibrant community.

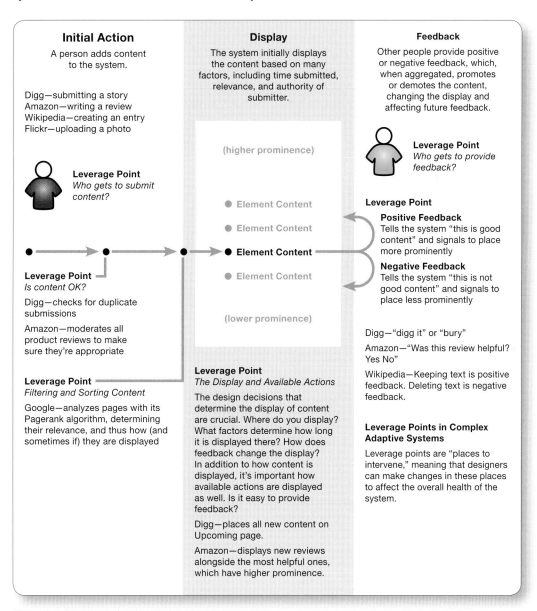

Initial Action

A person adds content to the system.

Digg—submitting a story
Amazon—writing a review
Wikipedia—creating an entry
Flickr—uploading a photo

Leverage Point
Who gets to submit content?

Leverage Point
Is content OK?

Digg—checks for duplicate submissions

Amazon—moderates all product reviews to make sure they're appropriate

Leverage Point
Filtering and Sorting Content

Google—analyzes pages with its Pagerank algorithm, determining their relevance, and thus how (and sometimes if) they are displayed

Display

The system initially displays the content based on many factors, including time submitted, relevance, and authority of submitter.

(higher prominence)

● Element Content

● Element Content

● **Element Content**

● Element Content

(lower prominence)

Leverage Point
The Display and Available Actions

The design decisions that determine the display of content are crucial. Where do you display? What factors determine how long it is displayed there? How does feedback change the display? In addition to how content is displayed, it's important how available actions are displayed as well. Is it easy to provide feedback?

Digg—places all new content on Upcoming page.

Amazon—displays new reviews alongside the most helpful ones, which have higher prominence.

Feedback

Other people provide positive or negative feedback, which, when aggregated, promotes or demotes the content, changing the display and affecting future feedback.

Leverage Point
Who gets to provide feedback?

Leverage Point

Positive Feedback
Tells the system "this is good content" and signals to place more prominently

Negative Feedback
Tells the system "this is not good content" and signals to place less prominently

Digg—"digg it" or "bury"

Amazon—"Was this review helpful? Yes No"

Wikipedia—Keeping text is positive feedback. Deleting text is negative feedback.

Leverage Points in Complex Adaptive Systems

Leverage points are "places to intervene," meaning that designers can make changes in these places to affect the overall health of the system.

Figure 6.11 Leverage points in complex adaptive systems.

Leverage Points

Donella Meadows, who founded the Sustainability Institute, wrote a paper called "Leverage Points: Places to Intervene in a System."[11] In this paper, she describes leverage points as "places in a complex system (a corporation, an economy, a living body, a city, an ecosystem) where a small shift in one thing can produce big changes in everything."

I first heard about leverage points from Gene Smith's Atomiq blog,[12] where he made the connection between Digg and Meadows' work, suggesting that "any large-scale social software application... is bound to resemble a complex system like an economy or ecosystem."

Many of the issues Meadows discusses, such as political and social points of leverage, are very much applicable to web design. My hope is that viewing web applications as complex social systems will help us reframe the design debate toward building healthy ecosystems, which will lead us to make more effective design choices.

Conclusion

The circumstances that led Digg to remove the Top Diggers feature last year were fascinating, a result of the hidden complexity of a system that lives and dies by the activity of its users.

Complex, adaptive systems like Digg, Amazon, Google, and others are the ultimate design challenge. Not only are their interfaces constantly changed by the addition of new content, but they are constantly being revised by the activity of their users as well. Despite our desire for design solutions that last, what works one day in adaptive systems might not work the next.

The goal of these systems is lofty: to elicit collective intelligence out of an undistinguished multitude. They do this by providing feedback mechanisms in which people promote the best content to the top, and send the worst content to the bottom.

The designers' role in these systems is never-ending. They must continually tweak the leverage points of the system, hoping to feed the growth of the community. All this while its members collaborate, collude, and act unpredictably. The only constant in these systems is change.

---

11 http://www.sustainabilityinstitute.org/pubs/Leverage_Points.pdf

12 http://atomiq.org/archives/2006/09/leverage_points_in_digg.html

Design for Sharing

How to build features that enable word of mouth

"There is no delight in owning anything unshared."

—Seneca, Roman Philosopher

In his book *The Tipping Point,* Malcolm Gladwell describes a rare type of person he calls a "connector." Connectors play a special role in society: they act like hubs of a network, spreading information from one node to another. They are the social conduit that keeps everyone up to date and informed.[1]

The main role of connectors is to spread ideas. They have wide social circles—much wider than the average person—and when they get excited about a new idea, they share it with everyone they come into contact with. That's just the way they are. Connectors love to be the first to tell their friends about a great new thing. They gain social capital as they do this. Their reputation grows. Their goal is your goal: to spread the idea. As Gladwell would say: connectors share information like it's a disease. And if that sharing reaches epidemic levels, you have yourself a tipping point.

---

1   Malcolm Gladwell, *The Tipping Point*. Back Bay Books, 2000.

Connectors are key enablers of word of mouth: they're super sharers. And to anyone building a social web application, they are like gold. If you can get a connector to talk about your application, then it stands a better chance of success, because more people will find out about it.

Of course, not everyone is a connector. Only a small number of people are going to go really nuts and tell everyone about you. By designing for connectors, however, we can support anyone who wants to share, whether it is a one-time event or one in a long line of shares.

Sharers are great for several reasons:

- ▶ **Sharers advertise for you.** When sharing works well, other people are doing a very important function for you: advertising. You don't have to spend as much money on regular advertising or other forms of attention-grabbing if sharers are spreading your word.

- ▶ **What sharers say is more powerful than what you say.** No matter how well you communicate the value of your application, it's not as powerful as something a sharer (or any fan) can say about you. If someone says, "that service is great, I highly recommend it," there is little you can do to improve on that message.

- ▶ **Sharers tell you why you're great.** Sometimes what a sharer says about you is different than what you say about yourself. Listening to them can give you insight into why other people get passionate about your application. Then in your future communications, you can emphasize those particulars.

The ultimate goal of designing for sharers is a virtuous cycle of sharing, where people who are happy using your application tell other folks who haven't yet entered the fold. They become sharers, and before long you have a sharer factory.

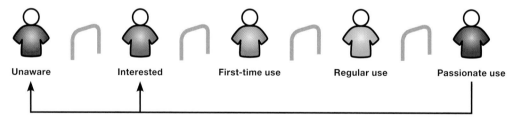

Unaware   Interested   First-time use   Regular use   Passionate use

Figure 7.1 Sharing is a great way for the passionate people using your software to spread their enthusiasm to folks who haven't yet tried it.

Why do we share?

There might be an evolutionary reason why we share: *to help our species survive.* But sharing is not just about survival, it's also about enjoyment and social standing. (Which, I suppose, could also argued are ultimately about survival, when all is said and done.)

Consider:

▶ In periods of scarcity, it makes sense to share resources so that more people can stay alive.

▶ In periods of plenty, sharing still makes sense, as it trains us to be more efficient with our resources. When tough times do come, they won't be so tough.

▶ We often share to enjoy similar experiences with others.

▶ Sharing allows us to show our affection for others.

▶ We can improve our social status by sharing. Those who share will be seen in a more positive light than those who don't.

▶ We sometimes anticipate reciprocity when we share. We assume that when we share something, we'll get something in return at a later date.

Sharing is a core part of ourselves: a core part of our identity. What we share and who we share it with goes a long way to explaining who we are as people. And though it might in the end be about survival, it is definitely a wonderful part of the human experience.

Two Types of Sharing

Sharing on the web generally falls into one of two camps.

Implicit Sharing

Implicit sharing happens when an item is shared as a byproduct of participation. On Del.icio.us, for example, your bookmarks are shared by default, so that others can see them even if your original intention was to simply save it for later. This provides value to others without your explicit decision to do so.

Explicit Sharing

Explicit sharing is how we usually share: on purpose. The most common way to explicitly share is by sending someone an email containing the shared item or a link to it. But now we're seeing many more ways to share. You can now send a shared item to your MySpace or Facebook account or submit shared items to social news services like Digg and Reddit.

Explicit sharing can be either one-to-one or one-to-many. When you send an email to a single recipient, it's one-to-one and therefore private. When you send an email to many recipients, or share an item with a social networking service, it's one-to-many and often public. Explicit sharing is what we're focusing on in this chapter.

Do Sharing Features Work?

Wait a minute, you say. This all sounds well and good, but isn't this overkill? When the content is good, won't people share things no matter what? Shouldn't we focus on creating great content, instead?

This is a fair concern, and the answer is YES! There is nothing more powerful than great content and a compelling experience. If you had to choose between focusing on content and focusing on sharing features, you should definitely focus on great content.

However, this isn't a zero-sum game. Most teams have both content producers and designers. So it's OK for designers to focus on creating sharing features. Even better, the designers and content producers should work together to come up with the best possible display for information.

Furthermore, it does help to prompt people to share. Consider this comment by Gina Trapani, editor of the popular blog Lifehacker, responding to a blog post where folks questioned whether sharing features even work at all while calling for specific evidence of their effectiveness:

> Actually, Lifehacker's traffic has gone through the roof since we started placing the Digg button on select featured posts. We go in and out of the Technorati top 10 regularly (at number 11 right now.)
>
> Forgive me if this sounds like horn-tooting. I bring it up only because you asked for evidence. Here it is.[2]

---

2   http://www.37signals.com/svn/posts/93-its-the-content-not-the-icons

As with any design concern, good judgment is best. Focus on a small number of effective sharing features for your sharers, and they will share more.

What to Share?

Here are just a few things you can share online:

news articles, blog posts, web pages, videos, pictures, wish lists, music, documents, calendars, reading lists, bookmarks, slideshows, spreadsheets...

Of course, this list isn't exhaustive; almost any digital object can be shared. Your design might introduce a new type of digital object that can be shared. For example, when Slideshare.net was launched in 2006, they made it simple and easy to share slideshows.

What do people like to share?

People share almost anything: living spaces, food, ideas. What determines whether or not something is shared?

It depends on the person, of course, but in general people tend to share:

- ▶ Ideas that reinforce what we already believe (belief perseverance)
- ▶ Ideas that surprise us
- ▶ Ideas that help explain something we already know (causation)
- ▶ Things we know another person will find valuable
- ▶ Useful tools—anything that makes a tough task easier
- ▶ Fun things like pictures and videos
- ▶ Things that make us look good

The Activity of Sharing

Sharing is a simple activity made up of several steps. For design purposes it helps to break it down and examine each step. Here's what a typical sharing process looks like:

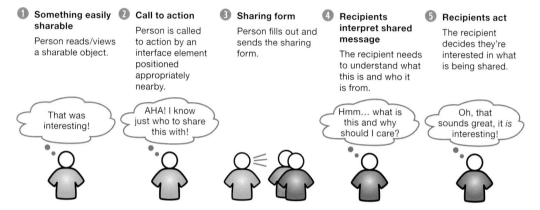

1 Something easily sharable
Person reads/views a sharable object.

2 Call to action
Person is called to action by an interface element positioned appropriately nearby.

3 Sharing form
Person fills out and sends the sharing form.

4 Recipients interpret shared message
The recipient needs to understand what this is and who it is from.

5 Recipients act
The recipient decides they're interested in what is being shared.

Figure 7.2 It's easier to design for sharing when you break it down into separate steps.

In the following sections we go through each step, talking about the design considerations that affect each one.

Sharers Discover Something Easily Sharable

The first step in the sharing process is someone discovering an item worth sharing. Sharing works best for distinct items like movies, songs, articles, and blog posts. These are perfect for sharing.

Here are some ways to make something easily sharable.

▶ **Give it a permanent URL.** URLs are core to the web. Give your item a URL and then people can refer to it anywhere. And never, never change that URL. For a rundown of the intricacies of URL creation, read Tim Berners-Lee's "Cool URLs don't change."[3] (You won't believe the gory technical details—or the benefits—of writing a good URL. For example, writing better URLs will actually get you better search result placement!)

▶ **Make it embeddable.** In addition to giving the item a permanent URL, make it embeddable, as long as it makes sense to do so. This was key to the explosive growth of YouTube. Social objects are the

---

3   http://www.w3.org/Provider/Style/URL

easiest to embed, like YouTube videos, Flickr photos, and Slideshare slideshows.

▶ **Make it a PDF.** PDFs are interesting things. They create the impression that their contents are more valuable than other formats like HTML pages. It's not entirely clear why, but people do love to share them.

▶ **Make it printer-friendly.** Make your content printer-friendly so that people can print it out and give it to others.

Sharers Heed the Call to Action

The call to action can be an interface element that signals the ability to share an item with others. In many cases the call to action will be the nudge that gets people to share.

Articles on the *New York Times* web site contain a typical set of calls to action for sharing news articles.

Notice the designers at the *Times* have separated out the one-to-one "E-Mail" option rather than including it under the list of "Share" options (even though they are both for sharing). Most sites and apps group these together.

YouTube is one such example. Their share feature is located directly under each video, and combines email sharing with sharing to services under a single "Share" link.

Figure 7.3 The sharing call to action on the *New York Times* web site (nytimes.com).

Figure 7.4 The sharing call to action on YouTube (youtube.com).

Of course, some people might share without using the feature you've provided. That's OK—you don't need to force people to use your tools (just be thankful they're sharing in the first place). However, as in most interaction design, prompting people helps: by providing a clear call to action, you make it much more likely to happen, and you do remind folks who didn't know it was an option or don't have an immediate need for it.

Keep the Call to Action Close

Increase the odds of sharing by placing the call to action close to the thing being shared.

One of the more innovative ways to keep the call to action close is to do what YouTube has done: actually replace the content with the sharing element. When a video is done playing, the view area is replaced by several features, including a share button. This draws extra attention to the feature.

CSI: Jim Carrey

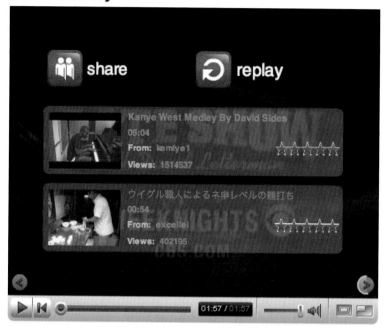

Figure 7.5 YouTube cleverly puts a call to action in the place where the video was playing.

Articles, unlike videos, don't have a time dimension. So the *Times* places their sharing box immediately to the right of an article, actually cutting into the article itself. This makes it hard to miss.

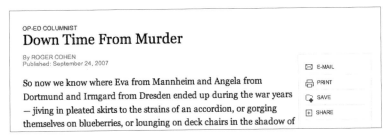

Figure 7.6 The *New York Times* places their call to action appropriately close.

Contrast the *New York Times* layout with *Wired* magazine's, which places the sharing tools farther up on the right of the page. These are not easily seen in the normal flow of reading, as they are above the horizontal line created when someone starts reading the article. (I actually looked around for a while before I found them here, as their position in the right column separates them unexpectedly.) Unless readers are proactively looking for them, they may not see them.

Figure 7.7 *Wired's* call to action isn't quite close enough to appear related.

Another alternative to placing the toolbar to the side of the article is to have a horizontal toolbar just below the article head. If it is distinctive enough yet not visually heavy, readers can quickly scan over it, see what's there, and not be distracted. Figure 7.8 shows an example from a site I designed called Publishing2.com.

Figure 7.8 Publishing 2.0's call to action, in the regular flow of reading but distinguished stylistically.

Time It Right

You'll notice that the sharing call to action on the *Times* site is at the top of the article, where it supports two contexts.

1. People who have just started reading
2. People who are returning to the article at some later point

This placement leaves a crucial context underserved: what about the people who have just finished reading the article? People who have just finished reading an article are the most likely to share, and the most qualified, since they have just finished getting value from it. Now they are ready for a new task. Yes, they might scroll back to the top, but many times they won't, and sometimes the top of the article will be on a different page. So place the call to action at the end of the article as well, where it is most timely. (It's perfectly fine to have a share feature in two places.)

Blogs tend to get this right, and offer sharing features at the end of articles. A good example is the bottom of articles on the GigaOm blog.

Figure 7.9 For maximum effectiveness, place a call to action at the end of content.

Give Options for Sharing

While email is the primary way of sharing, people are using lots of tools to manage their online content as well. These include bookmarking services like Del.icio.us and Ma.gnolia, social news sites like Digg and Newsvine, as well as social network sites like Facebook and MySpace.

For example, at Seth Godin's blog, lots of people used the Del.icio.us link at the bottom of each post to save his blog entries (the number of saves is displayed). Providing support for the larger of these services makes sense, as there's a good chance readers will be familiar with them.

It would also make sense to support tools that you know your audience happens to use. A good example is on an intranet: lots of intranets now have their own bookmarking tools, so supporting "Save" features for those makes sense.

Don't go overboard

In the excitement of providing options for sharing, it's tempting to offer every option. This happened on blogs, where some designers created a set of options for sharing that included, in some cases, dozens of applications. The result was a set of icons that simply overwhelmed.

Figure 7.10 When calls to action get out of hand.

Notice that the call to action is severely weakened with a long array of icons. Since there are so many icons, it doesn't make sense to include text, which is often the most powerful call to action. Therefore, this design leaves it up to the viewer to pick out their service by recognizing the icon, which may be difficult.

Sharers Use the Sharing Form

The sharing form is the form people must fill out in order to specify with whom they wish to share.

Here is a typical sharing form that I designed for UIE.com.

Figure 7.11 A sharing form from UIE (User Interface Engineering).

This form contains four form elements: two input boxes, one textarea, and the submit button. It's a simple form, but only because we followed the universal principle of form design:

Don't ask for any information other than you need.

A good thing to keep in mind for any web form is to try to reduce the number of items you request—as much as possible. The only field absolutely required for sharing in most cases (this one included) is the recipient's email. With that single piece of information you can send the sharing email. Still, I added two more fields. Why?

Well, I added "your email" for two reasons. One was familiarity. My team wanted the share to come from a familiar address, so recipients would be more likely to read it. Two, SPAM. We could have used the email share@uie.com or something similar and forgone asking for the sharer's email, but with so much SPAM out there we decided that it was good to try to identify who was sending. Many SPAM filter programs are trained to allow email from friendly addresses.

I also added an optional "message" that people could use to write anything they wanted. We found this to be tremendously useful in creating context around the email. They could say something like "this is the article I was talking about," or "check out this viewpoint in regards to our current project," or something similar.

If there were no personal message option, the sharing wouldn't have been as valuable. However, I explicitly made this field optional so that it didn't slow down those folks who weren't interested in it.

Note: I could have made it even more personal by asking for each person's name. In fact, an earlier version I designed had those fields. However, the form seemed daunting for such a simple task, with quite a bit more friction than the above version.

IBM, on the other hand, asks for such information.

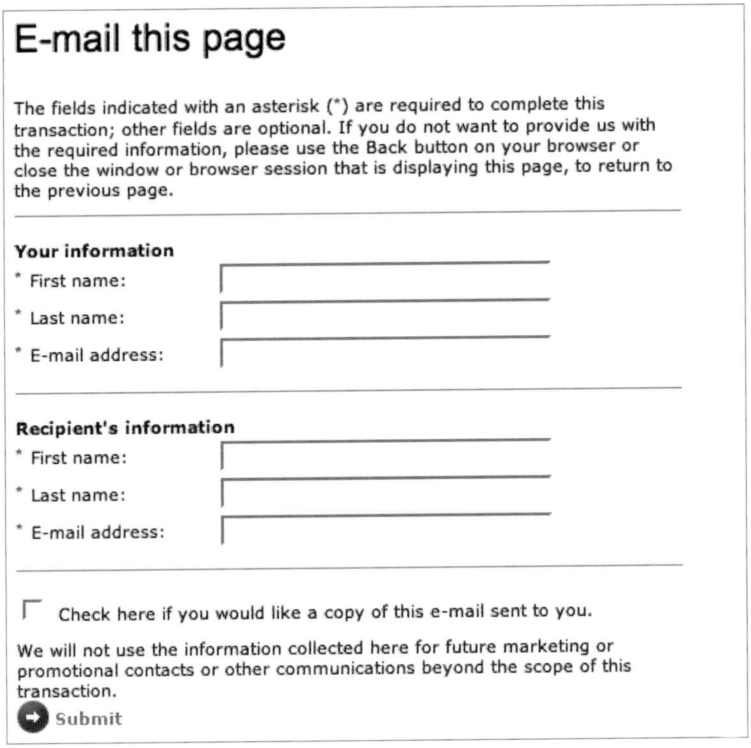

E-mail this page

The fields indicated with an asterisk (*) are required to complete this transaction; other fields are optional. If you do not want to provide us with the required information, please use the Back button on your browser or close the window or browser session that is displaying this page, to return to the previous page.

Your information

* First name:

* Last name:

* E-mail address:

Recipient's information

* First name:

* Last name:

* E-mail address:

☐   Check here if you would like a copy of this e-mail sent to you.

We will not use the information collected here for future marketing or promotional contacts or other communications beyond the scope of this transaction.

➡ Submit

Figure 7.12 The sharing form on IBM.com suffers several problems, one of which is that it looks like a test.

There are several problems with IBM's sharing form:

- **This looks like work.** With six fields presented all in a column, this form is daunting. The user came here wanting to simply send a web page to someone else, and this seems like they're taking a test.

- **Too many required fields.** There is only one field that is absolutely required to send this form! However, IBM makes all six required for submission.

- **Completely unnecessary fields.** Another thing, why does IBM ask for last names here? What value is it adding? For someone sharing a page with another, there is no reason to add a last name. You could argue that the sender's last name is possibly a good thing to ask, to make certain the receiver knows exactly which Robert is sending the email. But there is absolutely no reason to have the last name of the recipient.

- **Poor copywriting.** If you do need to explain what the form is about (and it's questionable in this case), reinforce the *value* of sending the form. The line "if you do not want to provide us with the required information please use the back button" does the opposite. There is no need for this explanation (obviously) and its presence raises concerns. Imagine if all forms on the web had that text! In IBM's case, their best hope is that people don't read the text! (The text at the end of the form is better: letting people know that their email is not being used for any other purpose is really important in this day and age.)

Give People Something to Do After Sharing

Don't treat sharing like it's the last thing someone wants to do. In fact, they might just be getting warmed up. Here is the follow-up message for the form I designed above. It clearly communicates that the sharing was successful, but also presents other options that might interest people on the site.

> ✓ **You have successfully shared this article**
> - Sign up for UIEtips to be emailed when a new article is published
> - Subscribe to the Brain Sparks RSS feed
> - Return to article

Figure 7.13 A note confirms that the sharing was successful. Follow that up with other options people can take advantage of if they're not done.

Remember, at this point the person is very special. They've just shared your content with someone else! Give them every opportunity to participate further.

Allow for Multiple Sharing

As we watched people share articles, we noticed that some people would share with each of their team members, one by one, creating separate emails for each person. This surprised us. We even had a few people share a single article seven or eight times!

Support multiple sharing. When the sharing process is complete, show the sharing form again near the place where you confirm success. Make it easy to share again: pre-populate with the message they already entered, so all the sharer has to do is change the name of the recipient.

Recipients Interpret Shared Message

How many times have you received an email from a friend or relative only to discover that it was one of those "forward me and you'll get good luck" emails? While we probably like that person, we don't appreciate their readiness to share this type of email with us. This is the sad state of sharing on the web. Even when people do share something with us, we still have to evaluate it just as we would any other type of information.

That's why the email sent during sharing is so critical. It needs to immediately signal to the receiver that it's authentic and worthy of their attention.

Consider the sharing email sent on MSNBC.com in figure 7.14.

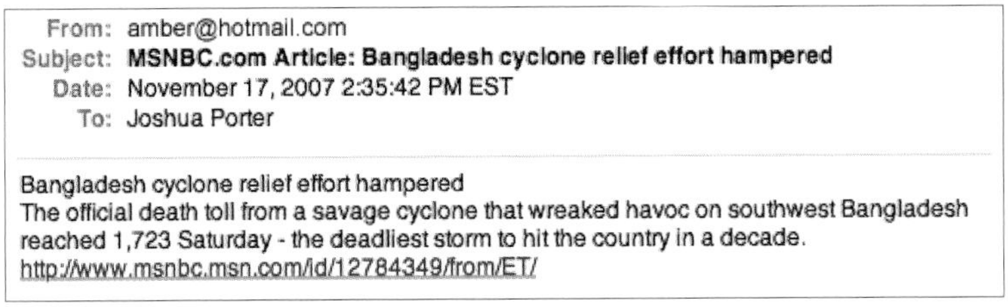

```
From:    amber@hotmail.com
Subject: MSNBC.com Article: Bangladesh cyclone relief effort hampered
Date:    November 17, 2007 2:35:42 PM EST
To:      Joshua Porter

Bangladesh cyclone relief effort hampered
The official death toll from a savage cyclone that wreaked havoc on southwest Bangladesh
reached 1,723 Saturday - the deadliest storm to hit the country in a decade.
http://www.msnbc.msn.com/id/12784349/from/ET/
```

Figure 7.14 An uninspired sharing email from MSNBC.com.

There are several problems with this email:

▸ **It looks like SPAM.** This email looks like SPAM, the kiss of death. Even though it is a completely legitimate email, it will likely be ignored.

▶ **It's not personal.** Other than the sender's email, there is nothing that identifies this email as being shared by two people who know each other. Part of the problem here is that MSN did not provide a message box in which sharers could write a personal message. Even if they did, they would still have to do something with that information in the email.

▶ **It's not authoritative.** MSNBC is a reputable news organization, and this email makes no effort to leverage that fact other than a mention in the subject line. Referring to the organization in the body of the email would lend more credibility to the message.

The email does do a good job of describing what the shared object is about. But that's all it does, and it risks being ignored.

The email I designed helped solve the above problems.

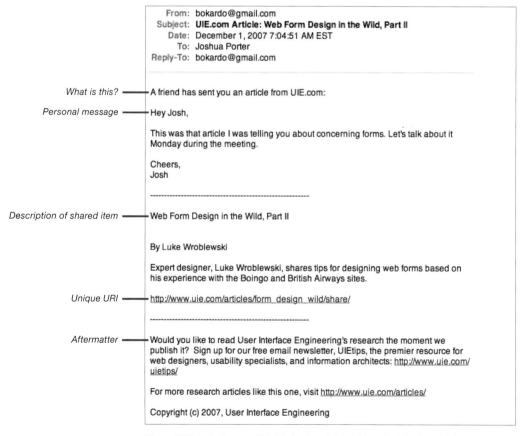

From: bokardo@gmail.com
Subject: **UIE.com Article: Web Form Design in the Wild, Part II**
Date: December 1, 2007 7:04:51 AM EST
To: Joshua Porter
Reply-To: bokardo@gmail.com

What is this? ── A friend has sent you an article from UIE.com:

Personal message ── Hey Josh,

This was that article I was telling you about concerning forms. Let's talk about it Monday during the meeting.

Cheers,
Josh

Description of shared item ── Web Form Design in the Wild, Part II

By Luke Wroblewski

Expert designer, Luke Wroblewski, shares tips for designing web forms based on his experience with the Boingo and British Airways sites.

Unique URI ── http://www.uie.com/articles/form_design_wild/share/

Aftermatter ── Would you like to read User Interface Engineering's research the moment we publish it? Sign up for our free email newsletter, UIEtips, the premier resource for web designers, usability specialists, and information architects: http://www.uie.com/uietips/

For more research articles like this one, visit http://www.uie.com/articles/

Copyright (c) 2007, User Interface Engineering

Figure 7.15 A sharing email that helps to set the right context for the recipient.

Once someone shares with someone else, that recipient has to recognize and interpret the thing being shared.

The More Personal It Is, the More Powerful

If possible, use both parties' names. This comes down to how much you know. If the person sharing is logged in, you probably know their name or other information already. Pre-populate the form with any information you know, and filling out the rest of the form will seem easier for them.

Also, it's OK to give people a message that is pre-written, as long as people can easily change it before it's sent out. Surprisingly, Amazon gets this wrong by providing a message that people cannot edit.

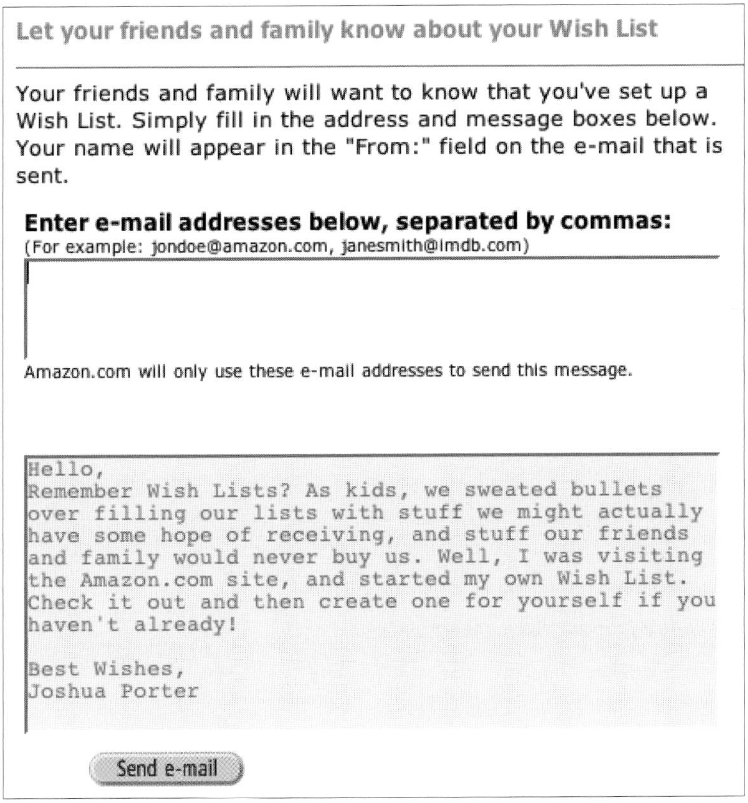

Let your friends and family know about your Wish List

Your friends and family will want to know that you've set up a Wish List. Simply fill in the address and message boxes below. Your name will appear in the "From:" field on the e-mail that is sent.

Enter e-mail addresses below, separated by commas:
(For example: jondoe@amazon.com, janesmith@imdb.com)

Amazon.com will only use these e-mail addresses to send this message.

```
Hello,
Remember Wish Lists? As kids, we sweated bullets
over filling our lists with stuff we might actually
have some hope of receiving, and stuff our friends
and family would never buy us. Well, I was visiting
the Amazon.com site, and started my own Wish List.
Check it out and then create one for yourself if you
haven't already!

Best Wishes,
Joshua Porter
```

(Send e-mail)

Figure 7.16 Amazon doesn't let you edit the message when you send someone your wish list.

Amazon has really gotten it wrong with this email, for several reasons:

▶ This form literally puts words into people's mouths, as they can't change the text.

▶ The copywriting is painful. It creates a fake history for the person and sounds like it was written by someone desperate to make a sale.

▶ It is obvious that nobody would write this to a friend. Do friends sign their last names? No.

Amazon's odd design choice to prevent people from personalizing the sharing email makes the act of sharing a wish list impersonal. Any advantage they could gain by allowing people to send it in their own identity is lost.

Recipients Act

The last step in the activity of sharing is that the recipients do something. If the sharer sent them an article, they'll read it. If it was a video, they'll watch it.

Presumably, you have already designed these objects to be easily used. But it's extremely important to pay attention to this act, so you can find out if the sharing is working. If a hundred people share your stuff, and only one is then using your application, it may mean there's a problem in the sharing process. Compare the sharing sends to the incoming actions. This percentage should be high—almost everybody. If the percentage is low, your email could be getting seen as SPAM.

Use Sharing Results to Inform What You're Doing

The *New York Times* has a list of the most-shared articles. It counts the number of times an article has been shared and ranks them over three time frames: the last twenty-four hours, the last seven days, and the last month.

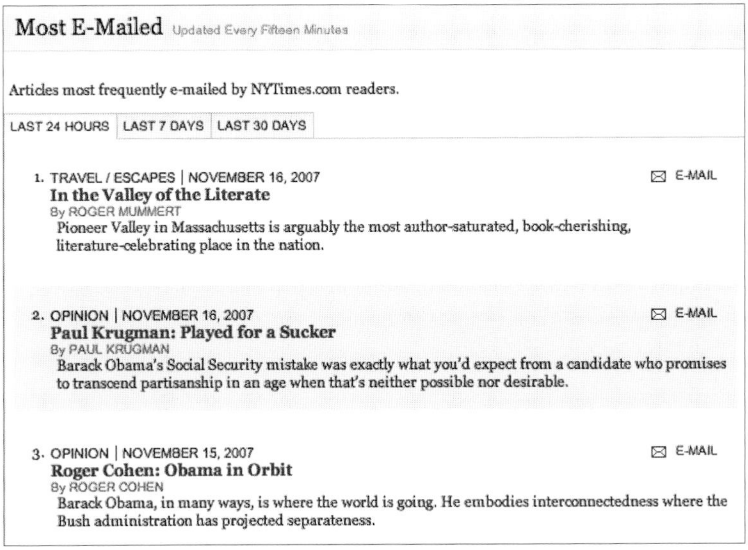
Most E-Mailed Updated Every Fifteen Minutes

Articles most frequently e-mailed by NYTimes.com readers.

LAST 24 HOURS | LAST 7 DAYS | LAST 30 DAYS

1. TRAVEL / ESCAPES | NOVEMBER 16, 2007 E-MAIL
In the Valley of the Literate
By ROGER MUMMERT
Pioneer Valley in Massachusetts is arguably the most author-saturated, book-cherishing, literature-celebrating place in the nation.

2. OPINION | NOVEMBER 16, 2007 E-MAIL
Paul Krugman: Played for a Sucker
By PAUL KRUGMAN
Barack Obama's Social Security mistake was exactly what you'd expect from a candidate who promises to transcend partisanship in an age when that's neither possible nor desirable.

3. OPINION | NOVEMBER 15, 2007 E-MAIL
Roger Cohen: Obama in Orbit
By ROGER COHEN
Barack Obama, in many ways, is where the world is going. He embodies interconnectedness where the Bush administration has projected separateness.

Figure 7.17 The *New York Times'* most shared screen. It's a great way to see what people are finding most valuable on the site.

This list is very valuable for the people using the site, who can use it to find the most popular content quickly, without having to search through each directory to find it. On a site as large as the *New York Times*, this is a real time saver.

In addition, the *New York Times* itself can learn a lot from a list like this. Not only do they learn what people find most valuable, but they can also track topics over time. Do some topics get shared more or less often? If so, the writers can use that information to plan future content around those topics people seem to enjoy most. By watching the trends that emerge in the sharing patterns over time, the *Times* can tweak its future content strategy when necessary.

Other Ways to Share

In order to highlight the five steps of sharing, we focused on sharing content with others. But there are other ways to enable people to help share their enthusiasm about your service with others.

▸ **Affiliate programs.** Affiliate programs let people who use your software share it with others by offering them a way to refer people. For example, Amazon has an affiliate program, which allows people to embed shopping links in their web pages that send surfers directly to Amazon's site for purchase. This drives more traffic to Amazon, while giving affiliates a small percentage of sales.

▸ **Simple Invitations.** Many applications offer a simple invitation feature. Facebook, for example, asks you to "Invite your friends." They allow you to import all of your addresses from web-based mail systems such as Hotmail, Gmail, and Yahoo Mail. This makes it easy for people to share their excitement about the service with others.

▸ **Testimonials.** As we mentioned in Chapter 4, Design for Sign-up, testimonials are a powerful way to expose the passion of the people who use your service. Leverage them not just for sign-up, but for all aspects of your customer-facing activities. Include them in emails, articles, and any other place where potential users might be hiding.

Perhaps the best way to have people share their enthusiasm about your application is to simply engage in dialogue with them. If they are passionate about your service, it will show through in their comments. Others will pick up on this and become interested as well. Passion is hard to hide.

Conclusion

Sharing is a fundamental human activity, and digitized content makes it easier than ever. Whether people are sharing news articles, recipes, pictures of their kids, or funny videos, they're helping to spread good will about your application, product or service.

So take advantage of the sharing tendency and enable those people who love to share. In some cases you'll get lucky and they'll be super sharers. Even if they aren't, their word is still gold, worth way more than anything you can say.

By focusing on the separate steps of the activity of sharing, we can design more appropriately for any given situation. By optimizing each step of sharing, we'll lose fewer folks along the way. Pretty soon you might just have a sharer factory on your hands.

The Funnel Analysis

A simple analysis tool to assess the health of your web site

"It is not the strongest of the species that survives, nor the most intelligent, but the one most responsive to change."

—CHARLES DARWIN

As we have noted through much of this book, there are important benefits to talking about your site in terms of the usage lifecycle.

In this chapter, we use the lifecycle to start measuring the effectiveness of your web site. It allows us to create a robust ecosystem for data-driven design.

The Funnel View

A good way to find out what's broken in your web app is a funnel analysis.[1] A funnel analysis can show how effective your site is at moving people along the usage lifecycle from Interested to Passionate.

So picture your site as a funnel. At the top of the funnel is everyone who is interested in your software. At the bottom of the funnel is everyone who is a passionate user of your software. Here's how it might look:

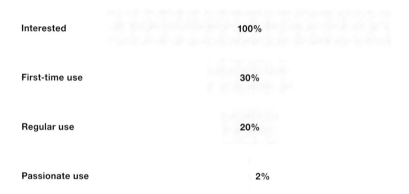

Interested	100%
First-time use	30%
Regular use	20%
Passionate use	2%

Figure 8.1 A conversion funnel for the major milestones in the progression of use. Having solid metrics for each of these steps is crucial to pinpointing problem areas in your interface.

The way to read this funnel diagram is as follows: of those people who get interested in your application, only some will actually use it for the first time. Of those people who use it once, only some will continue on and use your software regularly. Of those regulars, only some will become passionate users. Those passionate people make up only two percent of that original, interested group.

The key to the funnel analysis is the recognition that you will have leaks at every level. No matter how good your design, you'll lose people as they progress through your application. While it is *theoretically possible* to keep everyone from top to bottom, in practice you won't. There is no way around this: all funnels are leaky.

---

1   I learned the basics of this technique reading this article on funnel analysis by Mike McDerment (Mike knows his stuff: he's the CEO of the successful app Freshbooks): http://www.thinkvitamin.com/features/webapps/how-to-measure-the-success-of-your-web-app

Customizing the Funnel

The funnel in figure 8.1 describes a generic lifecycle of use for most web applications. However, to do an actual funnel analysis with real numbers you'll want to get more fine-grained with the levels of your particular application. Each site will have a slightly different funnel, as each site has a slightly different purpose, a different set of screens, and a different flow.

For example, "Passionate Use" is going to change depending on what activities your application supports. Passionate use could apply to someone who is a long-time paying customer or someone who creates lots of posts on their blog. Each site will be different.

To do an actual analysis, you need to figure out which metrics are important to you, and then construct a funnel made of those metrics.

The Analysis

For the following analysis, we're assuming a common scenario: a web site that allows for a trial period with upgrading to paid membership.

So let's reformulate our funnel accordingly. We now have five levels, particular to our scenario. In this example, "Regular Use," becomes "Paying Use," which is when people sign up, and pay for the service.

Site visit	100%
Trial sign-up	70%
Active use	50%
Paying use	35%
Recurring use	20%

Figure 8.2 This is a more concrete example of a funnel. By mapping these stages onto concrete metrics, we can get a clear idea of what's going on with our web app.

Using something measurable, preferably something whose meaning is obvious, create a metric to represent each level in the funnel. The following table describes each level in the funnel diagram.

Metric	What this means	How to measure
Visit	Visiting the site for the first time	Analytics program such as Google Analytics
Trial Sign-Up	Confirming a trial registration	Analytics program
Active Use	Logging in a certain number of times (five in a month, say)	In-house analytics
Paying Use	Completing a paid transaction	In-house analytics
Recurring Use	Creating several paid transactions	In-house analytics

Mike McDerment, the CEO of Freshbooks, describes the benefits of using in-house analytics for the lower levels of the funnel:

> We don't use our stats to track anything but the first two steps in our conversion funnel: visitors and trials…. I like the accuracy of database tracking—especially when your numbers are low (i.e. you are just getting started) and inaccuracies can really throw you off…. Also, and I would say this is much more important, analytics do not give you good active user counts. What does give you good active user counts is tracking the number of times a user logs in.[2]

With all this data to analyze, the question immediately arises: where do we see this information? How do we report on it? The most common way is to run periodic reports on your database by creating queries that expose the information. You run a query every week and analyze the funnel. Another alternative is to create an application dashboard that shows these numbers in real-time. (This type of management application is sometimes referred to as a shadow application.)

Discovering What Needs to Change

So now we have our funnel, and we're collecting data. We know what metrics we're going to capture. Now what?

How do we turn this data into actual design decisions?

The procedure for making changes is as follows:

1. **Create a baseline.** In order to know what numbers you're dealing with you need to create a baseline. This is simply the funnel data for the current design, *before* you make any changes. It's important to collect data for a baseline long enough so that you can tell when your number is being affected by spikes in traffic and when it is stable.

2. **Choose a level of the funnel to improve.** Do any of your baseline numbers look out of whack? A level that is especially leaky? If so, turn your attention there. If you don't see any glaring holes, then start at the top of the funnel. Changes there will have a bigger effect on throughput than changes on lower levels. Don't worry if the numbers are just plain weird at first. It may take a while to get used to your particular funnel. You might not even know what a leaky level looks like until you've used the analysis for a while.

3. **Investigate level for leaks.** If you are intimately familiar with your interface, you might immediately know what to address. Sometimes you'll look at a screen and immediately see a way to improve it. Other times, you won't. So find any data you can for that level: watch people use your software, talk to your community manager, pore over your support emails. Even the most polished software has little holes to fill. You'll find something to improve.

   If the level in question is made up of more than one screen, and your research into the problem isn't providing a clear answer, then consider doing a more fine-grained analysis. See the next section for an example.

4. **Make design changes.** Make a design change to the screen or screens on that level. Try to keep your changes relatively small, so that you can accurately tell if they had an effect. This is similar to setting up a scientific experiment: you only want to test a single variable in each test. On the web, development moves so fast that changing a single variable is often impossible. But it's better to make more, smaller, changes than a couple of big ones. You'll have a better idea of how well they worked.

5. **Measure change and compare to baseline.** Re-collect your funnel data after the change is made. You'll want to wait long enough so that you have a decent amount of traffic after the change. This will tell you if your design change had a positive or negative effect.

If fewer people are lost on that level of the funnel, then your changes were positive and you should keep them. If more people are lost, then you might consider rolling back the changes or making different ones.

6. **Rinse and repeat.** Repeat this sequence of steps until you can't improve your site any more (is that even possible?), or until the effort of making changes doesn't warrant the tiny improvements you're seeing. In general, however, there are always ways to improve *some* part of your application.

A Scientific Method?

Astute readers will notice that this set of steps loosely follows the scientific method. *This is no accident.* Like most things in life, the best designs do not spring from the head of their creator fully formed. They are the result of an intense process of trial-and-error, thoughtful evaluation, and endless tweaking. Successful designs rarely look like the idea they started out as; in the same way a finished statue barely resembles the block of marble it once was.

Audience Size vs. Length of Test

The time it takes to figure out how well a design change worked depends on the sample size of interactions. If your site is big and thousands of people are using it every day, then you can see the results of design changes faster. If your site is smaller, with fewer interactions, then you'll need to run tests longer to be able to compare against your baseline.

Huge sites like Amazon and Google, which have millions of visitors per day, have a distinct advantage here. They can run tests for very short periods of time and see clear results.

Getting Finer-Grained

Let's imagine for a moment that that funnel analysis told us to take a closer look at the "Trial Sign-Up" level. Unfortunately, sign-ups are often a multi-step process, involving several screens of our site as well as a confirmation email. If our data were pointing to a really leaky sign-up process, how would we know what to fix?

The answer is a to apply funnel analysis to a specific series of steps. Take the level that interests you and break it down into its own funnel for analysis. Here is an example:

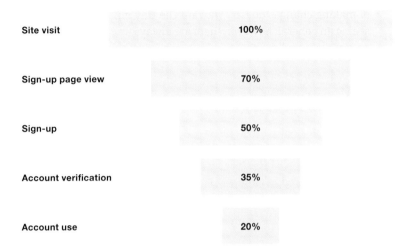

Site visit	100%
Sign-up page view	70%
Sign-up	50%
Account verification	35%
Account use	20%

Figure 8.3 Sign-up conversion funnel showing the steps you can measure. If one of these conversion rates isn't acceptable, you know where to change your design.

The goal with this finer-grained analysis is to break down the sign-up process into discrete steps. This is easiest if we can map screens to levels, where every screen in our application matches a level in the funnel.

Analyzing individual steps will allow us to pinpoint exactly what is wrong with sign-up. Is it the sign-up page? The sign-up form? Or the verification email?

Tip: Watch out for verification emails! They are notoriously leaky. I've had several clients whose emails were getting lost on the way to their recipients. Fixing that made a very big improvement immediately.

Social Funnels

Sign-up is a bugbear in almost all web applications. But there are other important funnels as well. Figure 8.4 shows a social funnel we can investigate to improve how frequently people are sharing your content. For more, see Chapter 7, Design for Sharing.

Of those people who read an article, for example, how many access the sharing form and send the article to someone else? I've highlighted in green the places where a second person is involved.

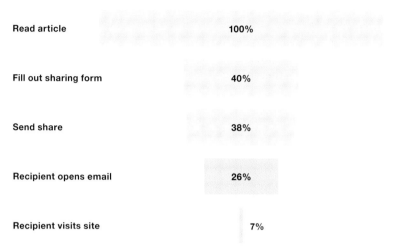

Read article	100%
Fill out sharing form	40%
Send share	38%
Recipient opens email	26%
Recipient visits site	7%

Figure 8.4 A conversion funnel for sharing. This involves two people, so the measurement is a little harder. I've highlighted the second person's activities in green.

Analysis During Change

There will be times when you want to make big changes to your design. You might get rid of screens altogether, either by getting rid of elements or moving them onto other screens. When this happens, you should evaluate whether your previous baseline is still meaningful.

If you change too many screens at once, the design will be so different that your funnel data won't be accurate. The numbers will be off, and your analysis will be distorted.

Here's how to make these changes. When you're making the big changes, expand your funnel far enough back and far enough ahead to measure things that won't change. Then set your baseline there, gathering enough data so that you're confident the numbers are stable. So, you're effectively changing the baseline *before* the change, which is crucial to the analysis.

Then, make your changes within the funnel, and watch the beginning and ending numbers. These will still be valid, while the numbers of the inside levels will be brand new.

The analysis for all funnels is the same. The important thing is to get as accurate a measurement as possible of each level.

You'll also note that design changes aren't always intuitive. For example, if you're sending out a sharing email and you add the shared content right in the email, you might get fewer visits to the site. However, if you don't add the shared content right in the email, you might get more visits to the site, but also more people complaining about it. Design is, in part, managing these trade-offs.

Issues to Watch For

Funnel analysis is a good way to get a handle on what's happening in your web application, but it's far from foolproof. Here are some issues to watch out for.

Faulty Baseline

The baseline data is crucial to good analysis. If you don't change your design, your funnel percentages shouldn't change much, either. Traffic will fluctuate, but your screens should have approximately the same throughput every day, in terms of percentage. If they don't, then get your data consistent before moving on to the other steps in the funnel analysis. It can take some serious investigation and tracking, but it's definitely worth it.

Different Sources Bring Different People

Part of getting a solid baseline is paying attention to where people come from. People from different sources act differently. If, one day, eight thousand people come to your site from Digg, they're going to skew your numbers. (Digg visitors are notorious for doing drive-bys, where thousands of people hammer your site for a few hours, mostly window shopping.) So make sure that you identify regular traffic and spikes in traffic to get cleaner numbers. This will help you get a better baseline.

Navigation is Non-Linear

Unless you're measuring a process with defined steps that must be completed in a specific order, your data is going to include people doing some odd things. People don't take a direct, linear path through your screens. Instead, they might click "back" a few times, reload a page, go to the home page and start over, or any number of other odd navigational behaviors.

This will add some noise to your numbers. They won't always make perfect sense. But being aware of how truly non-linear navigation paths are will help you determine when you're seeing normal behavior and when you're seeing something out of the ordinary. This is another reason why establishing a clear baseline is important. Most of all, you're looking for changes in traffic that correspond to design changes.

Size of Numbers

The numbers depend on your type of site. If you're offering a web-based tool, then your sign-up percentage should be higher than if you're running, say, Wikipedia. Wikipedia sees millions of visitors for every one that makes a change on the site. In general, if you provide free content that people don't have to sign up for, your percentages will be much lower than if your site exists to sign people up.

What are Reasonable Numbers?

The numbers I've shown so far might sound low, but they are very generous. Most applications will have much lower percentages. The numbers are different on every site.

Here is a table of actual numbers from feedback Mike McDerment of Freshbooks got. Notice that most are in the single digits. This is normal. Ninety percent of all visits are simply that—visits.

	Percent of first-time visitors sign up	Percent of sign-ups become paying users	Percent of paying users cancel each month
App 1	8.0	3.3	5.0
App 2	6.76	3.75	0.02
App 3	4.7	4.5	7.71
App 4	16.0	11.0	0.4
App 5	0.003	7.8	0

Hopefully, these numbers give you the impression that numbers can be quite small. The eleven percent for App 4 seems quite high here. But even changes in numbers this small have a huge impact if you're getting thousands of hits per day. On large sites, even a change of one percent can mean a huge increase in the population.

Tightening Your Numbers

The funnel analysis depends on accurate numbers. If you can accurately measure what's happening, you can make really solid design decisions. Here are a few ways to tighten your analysis.

▸ **Create landing pages.** Landing pages are special pages where people from a particular source land and start viewing your site. These pages are often specially tailored for the situation, with focus on a particular audience. People can't browse to them from your regular site. The key to landing pages is that they are shown only for very specific audiences. They may come from an email you send out, an advertisement on another site, or a specific link from your blog. Landing pages essentially segment your audience for you.

▸ **Measure sets of pages.** In the sign-up funnel as well as the sharing funnel, it makes sense to measure sets of pages at a level. So, for example, the "Site Visit" level on the sign-up funnel would include the homepage, a how-it-works page, and any other page that people learn from before reaching the sign-up page. In the sharing funnel, all the article pages on your site should be included, so if people share from any one of them, you'll know. This makes it easier to track funnels because you're allowing flexibility in the navigation paths of your visitors, but still getting the information you need for funnel analysis.

▸ **Segment your funnel.** Another way to improve the clarity of your funnel numbers is to segment general traffic into three categories: organic search traffic, direct traffic from other sites, and direct traffic (traffic with no referrals). This will allow you to get better numbers for each segment, and focus on those segments that are most valuable.

▸ **Use in-house metrics.** If you set up your own data-collection system, you'll know exactly what it is measuring. If you rely on a third-party system, you might get into guessing games about what the numbers mean, because you don't know the particulars of how they work and what they track. Invariably, if you don't control your own collection process, you won't know all there is to know about what you are measuring.

The worst way to measure your traffic is by third-party companies who aggregate traffic for the whole web. Their numbers just aren't accurate.

Marc Andreessen, who co-founded Netscape and is now working on social network site Ning, is very much against using these companies:

> You can't believe any of the Internet measurement companies for any kind of accurate external analysis of Ning usage and traffic—or, for that matter, usage and traffic of any web site other than perhaps the very largest.
>
> I'm talking about Compete, Quantcast, Alexa, and even Comscore— none of their data maps in any way to numbers or patterns we see in our own server logs and activity metrics.
>
> This is a well-known problem in the Internet startup world and isn't discussed often enough.[3]

Meaningful Metrics

The metrics that you use in the funnel analysis are crucial to success. If you weigh certain metrics over others, like prioritizing sign-ups over comments left on your blog, then your design will change accordingly. So it is key to choose the appropriate metrics.

The core analysis tool for processes on your site will be the funnel analysis. But for those things that aren't easily broken into a funnel view, you'll want a broader set of metrics to measure the health of your application.

The Death of the Page View

For many years page views were the primary metric by which traffic was measured on the web. As we mentioned in the opening chapter, in the beginning the web *was* mostly pages full of text. Now, sites have pages or screens with widgets, ads, or other elements that we've added over time. Page views have slowly become meaningless, for several reasons:

▸ **Always different.** Page views change depending on how the site is designed. For example, many online news sites split stories up on several pages to increase ad impressions, although others don't. Making any sense of page views is incredibly difficult for this reason.

---

3   http://blog.pmarca.com/2008/01/porn-ning-and-t.html

▶ **Ajax.** Ajax-enabled interfaces dramatically reduce page views because they allow developers to refresh parts of a page without reloading. If one site uses Ajax and another doesn't, the one that doesn't will have up to an order of magnitude more page views.

▶ **RSS.** RSS also changes the value of page views. If your readers are accessing content via RSS, then their views aren't counted as page views even though they're still reading the full content. If you provide RSS through your application, then your page view numbers will not reflect actual content consumption.

For all these reasons, the page view metric is no longer useful or widely used. Page views are more of an artifact of design choices than an indicator of success. The way you build your site, the technologies you use, and the way you distribute content shape the page view numbers so that they no longer represent a true picture of the people visiting and viewing pages.

Common Metrics

This far-from-exhaustive list can help get you started investigating metrics. You might just discover a metric for your own application that makes more sense than any of these.

▶ **Unique visitors.** Measures the number of unique people who visit. This metric gauges how many people are visiting, but gives no insight into what people are doing once they are there.

▶ **Repeat visits.** How often people return to your site. A high number of repeat visits suggests that people are well-engaged.

▶ **Time on site.** Time on site is the amount of total time a person spends on a site. High numbers may automatically seem better, but there are exceptions. Google, for example, doesn't want time on site to be very high. They want people to find the best search result as soon as possible—repeat visits is what they're after.

▶ **Pagerank.** Pagerank is the metric created by Google that informs their measure of relevancy for your site. The higher your pagerank, the more relevant Google thinks your site is. Since Google is a powerful force on the web that can send a lot of traffic your way, pagerank cannot be ignored.

▶ **Sign-ups.** Number of sign-ups. A high number of sign-ups suggests that your design is doing well to convince people that your app is worth it.

- **Feed subscribers.** Number of people subscribed to a feed (usually to a blog feed). This is a good indicator of how much attention you are getting.

- **Clickthrough.** When your site sends traffic to other sites, it makes sense to count the number of clicks. Google and other search engines do this to measure how effective their ads are. Clicks in general are more accurate than page views, but still suffer from being gamed.

Social Metrics

There are also many social metrics that measure user engagement. These include comments left, number of items shared, number of friends, number of blog posts, number of feedback messages, number of saved-to-favorites, number of bookmarks, and many others. The relative importance of each metric will vary according to what your application is built to do.

Activities Define the Important Metric

No matter what metrics you choose, you'll probably have a short list of extremely important ones. You may even only have a single metric that defines what you do.

Evan Williams, co-creator of Blogger.com, one of the first blogging applications, explains why the Blogger team focused on the number of posts as the important metric for success:

> At Blogger, we determined that our most critical metric was number of posts. An increase in posts meant that people were not just creating blogs, but updating them, and more posts would drive more readership, which would drive more users, which would drive more posts.[4]

Notice that there are several things going on here. Returning traffic (often split out as its own metric) is implicit in this metric, as people who post more will come back to their site more. Also, Evan assumed that more

---

4   http://evhead.com/2006/08/pageviews-are-obsolete.asp

posts meant more readers, which isn't *necessarily* true but *pragmatically* so. Your application will no doubt have its own intricacies. Identify what activities are most important for your population, and pay attention to metrics that measure them.

Conclusion

The funnel analysis makes each stage of the usage lifecycle concrete by explicitly calling out metrics that drive adoption and success. Each web site will be slightly different, but once you get your baseline metrics in place, you can confidently measure and make changes going forward.

Yes, there are a lot of steps that each person goes through in using your application. What the funnel analysis helps illustrate is that each step is no less important than those that come before or after it, because each step must be completed in turn.

Index